Importing Oxbridge

IMPORTING OXBRIDGE

English Residential Colleges and American Universities

ALEX DUKE

Yale University Press   New Haven and London

Library of Congress Cataloging-in-Publication Data
Duke, Alex, 1958–
Importing Oxbridge : English residential colleges and American
universities / Alex Duke.
        p.   cm.
Includes bibliographical references (p.   ) and index.
ISBN 0-300-06761-5 (alk. paper)
1. Universities and colleges—United States—Administration—History—
Case studies.   2. Educational innovations—United States—Case studies.
3. University of Oxford—Administration.   4. University of
Cambridge—Administration.   I. Title.
LB2341.D787   1996
378.1'5—dc20   96-16980
                    CIP

Designed by Sonia L. Scanlon
Set in Caslon type by Tseng Information Systems, Inc.,
Durham, North Carolina.
Printed in the United States of America.

A catalogue record for this book is
available from the British Library.

The paper in this book meets the guidelines
for permanence and durability of the Committee
on Production Guidelines for Book Longevity of
the Council on Library Resources.

10 9 8 7 6 5 4 3 2 1

To the memory of my father,
Irving Duke, 1926–1995

"Why are you making exhaustive researches into the social aspects of Oxford life? It takes an American to do that really well, you know."

"But what is the essential Balliol?" Michael demanded.

"Who could say so easily? Perhaps it's the same sort of spirit, slightly filtered down through modern conditions, as you found in Elizabethan England."

—Compton Mackenzie, *Sinister Street*

Contents

Acknowledgments

Working on this book reinforced my belief that there is no such thing as truly independent research, or at least good independent research. This study, judgments on its quality notwithstanding, reflects in a large and, I hope, obvious way the contributions of others, both academic and personal.

First and foremost I would like to thank William Reese, who directed the Indiana University dissertation from which this study is derived and provided critical input on subsequent drafts. Bill spent a great amount of time reading and offering suggestions, always with good cheer and abounding words of encouragement. I would also like to thank the other members of my dissertation committee, George Kuh, Jeanne Peterson, and Philip Chamberlain, who were similarly thoughtful, insightful, and supportive in reviewing my work. I am greatly in debt to other colleagues who read and commented on parts of my research while it was in progress. Harold Silver nobly read and critiqued three chapters while being driven across Indiana during a lecture tour; members of the Indiana University History of Education study group—including Ed McClellan, Robert Schwartz, Amy Schutt, Ted Stahley, Dick Rubinger, Ed Beauchamp, and Don Warren—also read and offered thoughts on portions of the manuscript. More recently, Elizabeth Whitt offered valuable suggestions on the the book manuscript. I am also thankful to Indiana University for financial support in the form of a Beechler Scholarship and a Graduate School Grant-in-Aid.

I would like to acknowledge a special debt to several teachers who made a lasting impact on the direction of my life, whether they knew it or not at the time. They are Allen Scholl, Barbara Cooper, Myrna Ziff, Steven Ort, Kenneth Kamp, and Herman Jay.

My thanks and deep gratitude go to Gladys Topkis and Heidi Downey of Yale University Press for their support and expertise.

On the personal side, I am most grateful for the moral and material support that my parents gave to me throughout my education and during the time I worked on this study. My only regret is that my father, to whom this book is dedicated, did not live to see it completed. Nevertheless, his encouragement and sense of confidence that things work out for the best remain with me always.

INTRODUCTION

Since the emergence of the modern American university in the late nineteenth century, educators have frequently expressed concern over the division of undergraduates and faculty into separate spheres. This issue, often associated with the growth of an institution and the increasing research orientation of its faculty, has been of particular concern in those universities that developed into centers of graduate education. A variety of tactics have been proposed to remedy this problem, but perhaps the most ambitious were efforts to establish systems of residential colleges within the university to provide a locus of out-of-classroom activity for both students and faculty.[1] A thread that linked these projects was their conscious reference to the organizational patterns of the University of Oxford, and, to a lesser extent, the University of Cambridge.

In the mid-1890s some Harvard University faculty members and alumni discussed the notion of reorganizing undergraduate education around small aggregations of students and faculty—fashioning it after Oxford's colleges—but the administration at the time, led by President Charles Eliot, did not share their interest. Two other university presidents, Chicago's William Rainey Harper and Princeton's Woodrow Wilson, were more receptive to residential college schemes, but they were nevertheless similarly unsuccessful in enacting such plans at their institutions. In 1902, Harper proposed that the undergraduate college at the University of Chicago be divided into eight quadrangles, each with its own faculty, students, and residential buildings; his death in 1905 halted these plans. Wilson's 1906 attempt to transform Princeton's undergraduate eating clubs into Oxford-style residential colleges met resistance from powerful rivals on the faculty and was ultimately quashed by that institution's trustees.

In spite of these failures, discussion of the idea itself continued into the late 1920s, when Harvard, Yale University, and Pomona College in California launched residential college projects. The financial support of Edward Harkness enabled Harvard and Yale to develop Oxford-inspired student residence systems, called colleges at Yale and houses at Harvard. At roughly the same time, Pomona officials adopted a plan to develop a system of autonomous residential colleges as an alternative to expanding within their existing unitary framework. Through this arrangement the college sought to preserve a small-college atmosphere while the school grew in size and mission. Beginning with the establishment of Scripps College in 1926, the Claremont Colleges, as the federation was named, expanded to five colleges and a graduate school.[2]

There was little new interest in residential colleges in the 1940s and 1950s, but the idea enjoyed a renaissance in the 1960s, when at least forty-four residential colleges were established at institutions across the United States. A national conference met in 1968 to discuss the future of the "cluster college" concept. Although these projects acknowledged several sources of inspiration, the cluster college proponents had "rediscovered the college structure of the venerable Oxford and Cambridge Universities," according to Jerry R. Gaff.[3] The largest undertaking of this movement was the establishment in 1966 of the University of California's Santa Cruz campus, which used the residential college as its principal organizational unit. Although the mission of UC–Santa Cruz would ultimately include graduate education and research, the master plan for the campus, mostly the dreamchild of University of California President Clark Kerr, called first for the development of a strong undergraduate base. The organization of the campus reflected Kerr's contention that the English university had elevated undergraduate education to its highest state. In the planning stages, the English influence on Santa Cruz's organization went beyond establishing a system of student residences: it was the college, not the academic department, that was to be the locus of faculty activity, with intercollegiate boards of study established to coordinate disciplinary course offerings at the campus level. Some planners even considered adopting the English model of comprehensive degree examinations.[4]

These projects took place against a backdrop of continual and often dramatic change within American higher education. Since 1860, every generation of American college alumni returned to alma maters that differed somehow from the institutions they had known as students. The most obvious manifestation of change was the increase in the student population. Although the climb in enrollments that followed the passage of the G.I. Bill of Rights in 1944 is well noted, the expansion in college attendance between 1870 and 1940 was no less dramatic. While the population of the United States tripled between 1870 and 1940, college enrollment multiplied thirtyfold. In 1900, there were 238,000 students in 977 colleges and universities. By 1920, there were 598,000 in 1,041 institutions. Twenty years later, in 1940, more than 1.4 million students attended 1,708 institutions.[5] In the post–World War II era, enrollments continued to skyrocket, though the growth in the number of new institutions later tapered off. In 1964, about 5.3 million students were attending American colleges and universities.[6]

As institutions of higher education expanded in number and size, the creation and dissemination of original scholarship became central to the mission of leading universities. In the nineteenth century, Americans traveled to Germany for advanced education in modern disciplines until such instruction became available in the United States in the 1860s. Professional research scholars who were educated in Germany or were taught along German lines at such institutions as Johns Hopkins University, had become a force in American colleges and universities by the 1880s. Armed with financial support from wealthy patrons and state governments, these educators rendered obsolete the practices of academics who believed that institutions of higher education existed to inculcate mental discipline and piety. By 1910, a Ph.D. degree was virtually a requirement for appointment to a professorship in a major university.[7]

As research gained importance in the growing institutions, so did the rancor of academic dissidents, who decried the so-called germanization of American higher education. The sentiments expressed in the early 1900s by such university leaders as Wilson and Harvard President A. Lawrence Lowell and by such journalists as Edwin Slosson and John Corbin held that the closeness between student and teacher was disappearing with this new emphasis on research.[8] Addressing this development a few decades later, Michigan professor of philosophy R. M. Wenley criticized the lack of faculty involvement in teaching undergraduates. Wenley believed that these students were "denied a vital source of intellectual passion by the very men whose prime duty it is to furnish it."[9] Although these words were spoken in 1918, they captured a sentiment that has persisted in large American universities to the present day. This dissent did not, however, diminish the importance of research to the professional academic. Throughout the twentieth century, the creation of knowledge increasingly determined the success of a university professor as undergraduate teaching conversely lost its priority. As Oscar and Mary Handlin observed, few scholars gladly assumed the task of rearing of the young; rather, it is the price of their freedom to pursue their own interests.[10]

Wilson and other educators saw the emulation of the residential traditions of Oxford and Cambridge as a way to reinvigorate undergraduate education in American universities. They believed that uniting students and teachers in small, semi-autonomous organizational units would resurrect the moral and intellectual role that faculty presumably played in undergraduate students' lives. Although none of the universities that experimented with residential colleges attempted to replicate the organizational pattern of their English models (although Santa Cruz came close, at least in the planning stages), all of them did aim to incorporate what they interpreted as the English residential college's essential characteristics. Besides residential-college schemes, some American institutions attempted to incorporate other aspects of the Oxbridge pattern, developing plans that included comprehensive examinations, pass and honors curricula, and a variety of forms of tutorial instruction.[11]

These efforts were consistent with a larger pattern of cultural association with England that the United States had maintained since achieving its independence, still referred to as the "special relationship." The American college of the early nineteenth century had tacitly acknowledged its English heritage, but associations with English culture and institutions became far more deliberate in the late 1800s and into the twentieth century. At that time, Americans visited Oxford and Cambridge in increasing numbers, usually forming lasting and positive impressions. Thus Oxford and Cambridge have "consciously and unwittingly . . . provided American higher education with symbols, forms, and vocabulary for much that is cited as the ultimate good in undergraduate education."[12]

The comments of A. D. F. Hamlin, a professor of architecture at Columbia, revealed the sense of reverence commanded by these institutions. "How potent," wrote Hamlin in 1925, "must have been the spell wrought through four centuries by the now venerable halls and cloisters of Oxford and Cambridge. How familiar and commonplace they must have become to the undergraduate rushing from lecture or quiz by his Don to the river or cricket field, and even to the fellows and tutors in their old halls. The quiet and century-old beauty of those ancient 'quads' . . . could not fail to become interwoven with the lives of the men who haunted them."[13]

The clearest physical evidence of this intensified interest in England was the popularity of Gothic Revival architecture in the United States, the style increasingly used in civic buildings, churches, and academic buildings. Beginning with Trinity College in Hartford, Connecticut, in the 1870s, many American college campuses adopted Gothic Revival architecture to link themselves more closely to their English cousins.[14]

This awareness of and responsiveness to the congenial aspects of Oxbridge were complemented by a lack of concern for the differences between American and English higher education. For example, the strong connection between Oxbridge and the upper strata of English society was inconsistent with the convictions held by many twentieth-century American educators (including conservatives) regarding higher education's role in the democratization of society. Oxford and Cambridge were bastions of privilege for much of their existence and strongholds of values and practices that many contemporary American educators deemed antithetical to intellectual and moral development. Indeed, a number of nineteenth-century English critics asserted that Oxbridge's exclusiveness and adherence to outmoded curricula had removed English higher education from the scientific and intellectual mainstream for more than two hundred years.[15] Even John Henry Newman, who found great value in the English collegial tradition, noted in 1852 that the tradition could easily inculcate intolerance and prejudice.[16]

Such concerns did not discourage proponents from their eagerness to emulate Oxbridge. Faced with the transformation of their colleges and universities into larger and less familiar institutions, these educators created an idealized picture of life in English universities. They saw in the collegiate structure of Oxford and Cambridge a way for universities to remain vital without sacrificing intimacy or faculty-student contact. By adopting the residential college structure—or some variant— American universities might once more offer undergraduates an educational experience in which the human element triumphed over the depersonalizing forces of an increasingly corporate world.

Those who championed the residential college idea in America generally did not base their understanding of Oxbridge on scholarly or even systematic study of the development of the two universities. Instead, they gleaned what was necessary to support their vision from popular notions and personal observations of Oxford and Cambridge, while ignoring or disregarding inconsistencies or contradictions. The content of these popular accounts of Oxbridge was consistent with a pattern noted by sociologist Burton Clark for institutional constituents to develop accounts of the past that embellish historical understanding in such a way as to smooth out conflict and contradictory trends in the stages of an organization's development so that it connects into a coherent and meaningful whole leading inevitably to the present. Clark called these accounts organizational sagas.[17] The organizational sagas put forward most often by denizens of Oxford and Cambridge— usually in the form of house histories, personal reminiscences, and fictionalized accounts of college life—offered a picture of slow change, ignoring or underplaying the dramatic changes that periodically affected both universities. The distorted view presented to American visitors suggested that the residential college was a stable, time-tested unit of academic organization whose adaptation to American institutions might remedy the problems associated with increased institutional size and the research orientation of faculty.

Sociologist Edward Shils drew a distinction between *noumenal* and *perceived* accounts of the past. The noumenal past is that which historians attempt to discover and construct. Although the noumenal past is never synonymous with objectivity, it nevertheless attempts to provide a critically defensible picture of what has transpired, with the author's values and assumptions made clear to the reader. In contrast, the perceived past relies less on critical defensibility and more on the significance that past events may have in providing meaning or explanation for current conditions or circumstances. The perceived past is, as Shils notes, more plastic than the noumenal, "more capable of being retrospectively reformed by human beings living in the present."[18]

In this book I show how efforts to create Oxbridge-inspired residential college systems at American research universities were grounded in this perception of English higher education. I further demonstrate how, once established, residential college systems were difficult to reconcile with the organizational mainstream of American higher education and generally did not live up to the expectations of their founders.

In the first chapter I offer a noumenal past of Oxbridge, focusing on the periods of intense reform that shaped the modern appearance of the two universities. This account of the development of Oxbridge is contrasted with the perception of Oxbridge popular in the United States in the late nineteenth and early twentieth centuries as having evolved through the ages. This notion led outsiders to believe that the residential college was a proven arrangement for uniting faculty and students in an intellectually engrossing atmosphere.

In the second chapter I explore the increasing attention paid to Oxford and Cambridge by American educators beginning in the late nineteenth century, and I examine how one group of these men—most notably Woodrow Wilson and Lawrence Lowell—advocated organizational reform based on the English collegiate pattern in order to remedy faults in American universities—flaws that were attributed to the influence of German research scholarship. This advocacy was based largely on a belief in the development of Oxbridge.

In the remaining chapters I recount American efforts to establish residential colleges in the twentieth century, exploring the influence of perceived notions of English higher education and the extent to which American schools succeeded in creating intimate communities of students and faculty. The institutions I selected for study were the sites of the best-known attempts to imitate Oxbridge in American higher education. They shared three other important features: First, the project planners clearly acknowledged Oxford or Cambridge (usually Oxford) as their source of inspiration. This condition excludes from my study an institution such as the Atlanta University Center (AUC), for example, whose federal structure resembled that of the Claremont Colleges in many respects but did not acknowledge Oxford or Cambridge as its model. Second, the proposed residential colleges needed to be small enough to approximate the scale of the English colleges, which rarely exceeded 600 students. Therefore, the study does not include such institutions as the University of California, San Diego, which was organized around cluster colleges comprising 1,500 to 2,500 students, most of whom were nonresident. Third, I consider only institutions that included a majority of the undergraduate student body in the residential colleges. Thus, Michigan State

University, which established three residential colleges in the late 1950s, was not included because its units housed and educated only about one-tenth of the undergraduate student body.

In Chapter 3, I recount unsuccessful campaigns undertaken at Harvard University, the University of Chicago, and Princeton University between 1894 and 1910 to create support for new systems of student residences modeled after the Oxford colleges. In Chapter 4, I detail how residential college ideas contributed to the creation of the Harvard house and Yale residential college systems in the late 1920s. I also show how the houses and colleges failed to meet the expectations set forth by their proponents, even though their presence did reestablish each institution's residential character. In the fifth chapter I chart the development of the Claremont Colleges (beginning in 1926), which grew out of an attempt by the president of a private college in Southern California to create a group of interdependent small colleges patterned after his personal vision of Oxbridge. In Chapter 6, I examine the planning and development of the University of California, Santa Cruz (1966), the most ambitious undertaking of the contemporary revival of interest in residential colleges.

I

The Paradox of the English
Residential College

In 1925, after three years of teaching American history at Oxford, Samuel Eliot Morison wrote that "no sensible man who knows Oxford would wish greatly to change it. Rather, he must be chiefly concerned to preserve the many things of worth and beauty that time has tested, and spared."[1] Morison agreed with what many Americans of his day considered common knowledge. As Edmund Burke attributed the superiority of English government to the accumulation and testing of experience over generations, so too had the English university come to embody the best elements of a long pedagogical tradition. But had Morison included a more probing account of the development of Oxford or Cambridge in his historical research, he might well have revised his understanding of how change occurred in English universities. As the works of later historians testified, the development of Oxford and Cambridge included as much tumult, disruption, and rapid transformation as did the development of higher education in the United States in the late nineteenth century, or after World War II.

These conflicting conclusions form the basis for two sharply diverging accounts of the development of early-twentieth-century Oxbridge. The first account is based primarily on the work of academic historians and can therefore, using Professor Shils' term, be considered an explanation of Oxbridge's noumenal past.[2] This interpretation holds that the collegiate structure and the belief in an ethos based on both the intellectual and social development of the student came after periods of intense reform and reorganization that involved change both within and outside the university establishment. In addition, this noumenal past attributes much of the social and intellectual development exhibited by Oxford and Cambridge students to factors that occurred beyond the scope of their university education or residential college experience. In short, this is the account of the development of Oxbridge that was missed by Americans and Englishmen alike in the late nineteenth and early twentieth centuries.

The other depiction of Oxbridge's past is the one more familiar to such American visitors as Princeton President Woodrow Wilson and journalist John Corbin, who became convinced that emulating English educational practices would provide a tonic to the changes that they felt had disrupted American undergraduate education. This *perceived* past made little mention of revolutions in the development of Oxford and Cambridge or of the influence of forces in English society that shaped the behavior and life course of Oxbridge students. Indeed, it was less a formal history and more a compilation of anecdotal understanding that emphasized the importance of centuries of continuity and stability, and an unbroken tradition of preparing men for civic life. The perceived past was reinforced by the anti-utilitarian views on education held by Victorian authors, chiefly John Henry Newman and Matthew Arnold. These beliefs were reflected in a new ethos of English university life that emphasized cultivating an intellectual and a cultural elite. In addition, university men themselves began in the late nineteenth and early twentieth centuries to write college and university histories that emphasized the distant past and said little about recent changes. Finally, popular literature about Oxford and Cambridge became steeped in the ideas of Newman and Arnold, perpetuating the concept that the university's atmosphere, developed over the ages, was the university's most potent educating force.

The Noumenal Past

Throughout the Middle Ages, Oxford and Cambridge largely resembled other European universities. Their curricula offered rigorous training in logic and disputational techniques useful for graduates who sought careers in governmental, judicial, ecclesiastical, and academic fields. Instruction, usually in the form of lectures and disputations, was provided primarily by regent masters, recent graduates who remained at the university to teach for a specified time. The corps of teaching masters was organized around four faculties, each corresponding to one of the major divisions in the curriculum. The largest of these groupings was the arts faculty, which provided the foundational education for the faculties of medicine, law, and theology. Although Oxford and Cambridge organized their curriculum like continental universities, examination policies differed markedly. The English university student was not required to take written examinations before his degree was conferred, because he (these were all-male institutions) was considered to have undergone evaluation throughout his academic career.[3]

Colleges played a limited role in medieval Oxford and Cambridge. Most students lived in boardinghouses, not in colleges. Called *aulae,* or halls, at Oxford and hostels at Cambridge, these were usually profit-making ventures that held from ten to eighty students.[4] Until the sixteenth century, founding a hall required only that a few scholars rent a house, provide a deposit to the owner, and choose a graduate of reasonable character to be principal. According to university statutes, the chancellor could not refuse to sanction a hall if these procedures were followed. Throughout the Middle Ages, there were always many more boardinghouses than colleges.[5]

In contrast with the boardinghouses, the earliest colleges were established as foundations to provide accommodation or financial support to students in the advanced faculties. Although these students were drawn almost exclusively from families of middling social status, they required economic support to remain at the university throughout their degree programs. Most of the English colleges were founded by ecclesiastical authorities or royal courtiers whose courts and households depended on university-trained clerks. The inspiration for these graduate colleges came from the Collège de Sorbonne at the University of Paris, which, according to Alan Cobban, was intended to be "a community of scholars with like minded interests who in theory, at any rate, were to live together in harmonious amity and in an environment of stimulating intellectual exchange; a Christian society embodying spiritual, moral and academic excellence."[6] Whether any college ever lived up to this ideal, most founders intended to provide an opportunity for advanced students to pursue their studies in a setting uncompromised by the normal vicissitudes of university life.

Although organizational practices varied from college to college, the pattern established in 1264 at Merton College, Oxford, proved enduring. In the Merton arrangement, the college was governed by fellows appointed from among the graduates; those fellows were supported by the endowment. Ultimate authority was vested in the corporate will of the fellows, but the officers of the college, usually elected from among the fellows, conducted the day-to-day business. Election to a fellowship was almost never based on open competition. College benefactors limited fellowships to their own kin, inhabitants of particular counties, students educated at particular schools, members of particular orders, natives of particular dioceses, and many other criteria. Once elected, a fellow continued to receive his income and enjoy his privileges, including a voice in college affairs, until he married, received a better-paying position, or died.[7]

By the middle of the sixteenth century the college-dominated federation that remains so closely identified with Oxbridge had supplanted the older university structure. The professional curriculum was gone as well, replaced by a classically based course of study. These changes were not the result of educational reform or innovation but were instead related to the efforts of Tudor monarchs to forge a centralized, consolidated state.

The suppression of the Catholic Church, which led to the creation of the Church of England in 1521, was the most critical event affecting this transformation. The assumption of religious supremacy by Henry VIII meant that the study of canon law no longer offered an avenue of advancement for those seeking positions of state. New opportunities now arose for laymen in government and resulted in a new kind of student arriving at the universities: sons of gentry or nobility who sought the chance to acquire the education—and the connections—needed to obtain a position in government. The new students saw university education as a means to tap into the network that existed between the university and scholarly circles, and the royal and religious households and courts. Consistent with these changes, the professional nature of the old curriculum, in which the arts were clearly subordinate to the higher faculties, was supplanted by a belief that the virtue and wisdom obtained in a literary education developed the abilities to manage affairs of state.[8]

The colleges were quick to grasp the advantages of adding these new students to their membership. A small number of undergraduates had lived in colleges in the pre-Reformation era, but the major departure came when colleges began to house large numbers of fee-paying students from more affluent social backgrounds. There were practical reasons for this change in policy. The confiscation of the Catholic Church's wealth in England forced many colleges to seek new benefactors and made the admission of fee-paying students desirable. Recognizing the special requirements of the sons of the wealthy and well born, the colleges increased their efforts to supervise the moral and personal lives of students. Fee-paying students were supervised in loco parentis by tutors chosen from among the resident fellows; their primary responsibility was to ensure that these students remained civil and met their financial obligations to the college.[9]

The sudden growth of the number of college foundations in the late fifteenth and early sixteenth centuries was accompanied by the decline in the number of halls and hostels. By 1552, there were only eight halls at Oxford. By 1573, Cambridge had only nine hostels, all of which were soon absorbed by colleges.[10] Part of the decline was attributed to the lack of endowments needed to sustain the boardinghouses through hard times, but the natural rise and fall of the student housing business was compounded by the expansion in the number and size of colleges.

As the colleges consolidated control over the student housing market, Tudor and Stuart monarchs, especially Elizabeth I and James I, found political advantage in facilitating the creation of a college-dominated university. Statutes passed in the mid-seventeenth century replaced the rule of the regent masters by an oligarchy consisting of the heads of the colleges. The concentration of power in a small appointed body enabled the crown to maintain leverage over the universities, which were intended to act as "engines of Anglican uniformity." The new governing bodies, Oxford's Hebdomadal Council and Cambridge's Caput Senatus, carefully looked after the interests of the existing colleges.[11]

The new form of governance was a political victory for England's rulers, but the accompanying political and religious interference retarded the development of the universities as seats of learning. The collegial monopoly, combined with the fellowship system, contributed strongly, in the minds of many critics, to the intellectual decline of the universities. As Mark Curtis notes, the decline of Oxford and Cambridge as intellectual centers came about because the English universities were closely connected to other political and social institutions and therefore came to reflect the religious intolerance and political suspicion that characterized English life under the Tudors and early Stuarts. The universities became so woven into the political fabric of English institutional life that their powers to control their own affairs and to initiate desired improvements "fell victims to intransigence from without and to hypocritical time-serving and complacency within."[12] The institutionalization of political and religious control, largely accomplished by the imposition of collegial oligarchies, resisted change and reform even when English political and social life began to show signs of toleration and renewed interest in intellectual development. What Curtis calls the "long academic depression" lasted into the nineteenth century.

Even though the universities remained wedded to instilling moral and mental discipline, scientific and philosophical advancement flourished elsewhere in Britain. This irony was not lost on some of eighteenth-century England's most famous thinkers, several of whom became outspoken critics of Oxford and Cambridge, including Oxford graduates Edward Gibbon and Adam Smith. Gibbon cheerfully expressed his willingness to disclaim his alma mater and called his years at Magdalen College the "most idle and unprofitable times" of his whole life. Smith charged that the intellectual malaise of the colleges had resulted in a conspiratorial neglect of duty by their fellows: "If instructors are only subject to their own corporate authority," wrote Smith, "they are likely to make a common cause, to be all very indulgent on one another, and every man to consent that his neighbor may neglect his duty, provided he himself is allowed to neglect his own." The criticism became even more intense in the early nineteenth century, when a series of articles published in the *Edinburgh Review* attacked Oxford pointedly, taking objection to the usurpation of the university by the colleges, the fellowship system, and, especially, the inadequacy of the curriculum to meet the needs of contemporary English society. One critic wrote in 1809 that the "young Englishman . . . has scarcely a notion that there is any other kind of [academic] excellence" than classical languages.[13]

In fairness, the curriculum of the universities had not remained entirely stagnant. Mathematics had been introduced into the Cambridge curriculum in the early seventeenth century and became the basis of the university's first honours examination. However, the allegiance of Oxford and Cambridge to their mostly classical curricula compelled many prospective university students to leave England if they they sought education in a wider range of subjects. Some of these students went to the University of Edinburgh in Scotland, but the University of Göttingen in the English-ruled Electorate of Hanover became a major center of advanced scholarship for Englishmen in the first half of the nineteenth century. Göttingen was founded in 1734 by George II, King of England and Elector of Hanover, to train ministers and civil servants for his German dominions. Many of Göttingen's original core of scholars came to the new university because they wanted to pursue a meaningful and humanistic approach to the classics. By 1820, Göttingen had widened its academic offerings to include natural science and bibliographic study. In 1824, when Thomas Hodgskin described the university in his *Travels in the North of Germany,* he noted that Göttingen possessed many more in-structors than did the English universities and that lectures were given on many more subjects. Academic renown in these fields enabled Göttingen to attract students from all over Germany, England, and the United States. Many of its professors were well-known Anglophiles, and the university was called "London in miniature." The relation between Göttingen and England grew strong enough that in the 1850s some students were allowed to submit their dissertations in English.[14]

As the reputation of Göttingen and other German universities became well known in England, the objections raised by critics concerning the state of domestic higher education intensified, particularly regarding Oxford. In the face of escalating criticism, Oxonians formulated a rationale to explain the value of a university education. Proponents of classical education now asserted that the purpose of the university education was to counter the effects of gross materialism and overspecialization; in essence, they defended the classics by attacking the educational suitability of practical or useful subjects. Edward Copleston, the rector of Oriel College, in 1810 set forth a major statement arguing against charges that classical education was impractical and pedantic. Classical literature, he asserted, "supplies common topics and kindles common feelings, unmixed with those narrow prejudices with which all professions are more or less infected." "Never let us believe," he continued, "that the improvement of the chemical arts, however much it may tend to the augmentation of national riches, can supersede the use of the intellectual laboratory, where the sages of Greece explored the hidden elements of which man consists." Copleston's defense was fortified by then-popular notions of faculty psychology, which held that the study of difficult and demanding subjects, such as Latin grammar and repetitive mathematics, strengthened the brain in the way physical exercise strengthened muscles. Copleston argued that logic, divinity, and mathematical theorems "discipline the reasoning power" and that such study "expands and enlarges the mind, excites its faculties, and calls those limbs and muscles into freer exercise."[15]

Beyond his rationale for classical education, Copleston irked critics by favoring Oxford's autonomy over its duty to be useful to the state. He asserted that Oxford was not really a national foundation at all but a federation of private endowments. To Sir William Hamilton in 1831, this attitude illustrated "how completely the *University* is annihilated—how completely even all memory of its history, all knowledge of its constitution, have perished." Hamilton and other critics demanded the restoration of the functions and privileges of the university—providing instruction and rigorous examinations—that the colleges had usurped.[16]

In the 1840s, men within Oxford, primarily tutors, joined external critics in advocating reform. Many of these new critics felt that that university teaching ought to be a serious and lifetime occupation rather than a way station on the path to a clerical career. Although disagreement existed concerning the relation between teaching and knowledge and between the value of teaching practical subjects or conducting scholarly research, these reformers collectively rejected the Coplestonian position that the universities existed to provide mental discipline and to inculcate religious values.[17] In the mid to late nineteenth century, these forces were able to draw attention to inadequacies in English higher education. As a result, reform—much of which required parliamentary action to overturn the existing statutes —came in many areas of university life. The most important changes concerned the creation of a new degree structure, an expanded curriculum, written examinations, and the development of university teaching as a profession. The reforms differed in timing and content at Oxford and Cambridge, but by the turn of the century the organization and programs of the two universities were very similar.

The basis for the modern system of written examinations and degrees took form at Oxford in the first decade of the nineteenth century, before the era of parliamentary intervention. Several Oxford colleges had initiated a bifurcated system of awarding bachelor's degrees that was closely connected to a new system of comprehensive examinations. To earn the basic, or "pass" degree, a candidate underwent an examination that covered a variety of subjects, though for a period this examination lacked rigor. In contrast, students seeking the "honours" degree, established in 1807, were tested more comprehensively on subject matter in a specific area. These examinations were oral until 1830, when they became primarily written. The first of the honours examinations was in classical literature, and seven other examinations were established during the nineteenth century. In the 1840s, examinations became increasingly important at Cambridge as well. Although mathematics still dominated the course of study at Cambridge, a classical examination appeared in 1822, followed by examinations in natural and moral sciences in 1849.[18]

Progress toward uniform implementation of examinations was accelerated in 1850 when Parliament passed the Examination Statute, which mandated that all candidates for a bachelor's degree take examinations in two schools: one in classics, which comprised political economy and ancient history, as well as Latin and Greek, and one in mathematics, natural science, or history and jurisprudence.[19]

The rising importance of examinations and the broadening of the range of examination subjects placed new demands on the teaching capabilities of the colleges and stimulated efforts to reform the tutorial system. Securing the assistance of a professional coach became increasingly important for students. Although the existence of these crammers embarrassed the universities, they nevertheless performed and a necessary role. Although several critics suggested creating a professorate along German lines, the prevailing belief was that responsibility for primary instruction should lie with the college tutors—that is, the fellows in residence. The ultimate success of academic reform, however, depended on turning university teaching into a sustainable career. The major obstacle to the establishment of such a profession was the fellowship system itself. As Sir William Hamilton observed, "The fellowships were not founded for the purposes of teaching, so the qualifications that constitute a fellow are not those that constitute an instructor."[20] The ban on married fellows was a significant barrier as well. In early-nineteenth-century Oxford, only about 10 percent of the positions in the colleges or university were open to married men.[21]

Some early progress toward reform was made at Oriel College, which opened its fellowships to the whole university in 1821 on the basis of academic competition. Otherwise, efforts proceeded slowly: by 1850 only 22 of 500 fellowships at Oxford were open to general competition. An overhaul of the system did not take place until 1877, when a Royal Commission of Inquiry mandated the creation of new collegial statutes. Many of these new statutes abolished life fellowships, making possible the appointment of tutorial fellows whose primary function was to instruct undergraduates. A number of college ordinances that followed the parliamentary action resulted in the suppression of fellowships and the establishment of endowment-funded professorships and pensions for retired fellows. Most of the new collegial statutes allowed fellows to marry.[22]

Many of the teaching reforms that took place at Oxford in the middle of the century were not duplicated at Cambridge until after 1860. Although the major issues, such as fellow-ship and statutory reform, were largely the same as at Oxford, change was more drastic because the state of teaching at Cambridge was reputedly even worse than at Oxford. Until the 1860s, Cambridge tutors did not teach undergraduates at all and were not even a conspicuous part of the colleges; they supervised the students in loco parentis, and students relied on private coaches for tuition. In the 1860s, however, a new group of dons emerged, distinguished by their professional interest in scholarship and conviction that teaching helped to develop character. The arrival of these new dons meant that students would no longer engage professional crammers to prepare them for examinations. Rather, they were instructed by tutors, within their colleges. The concept of individualized instruction was retained, but cramming was replaced with tutorial assistance. Many colleges vacated fellowships to establish teaching professorships. In attempting to interest students in serious scholarship, these new dons opened up their personal lives to students to an unprecedented degree, though they clearly favored honours men. Cambridge rescinded the restrictions on married fellows in 1882.[23]

A new system of secondary education emerged in the mid-nineteenth century to supply the reformed universities with students ready to pursue specialized scholarship. Consisting of medieval and reformation-era establishments, such as Eton and Winchester, and a number of institutions founded in the nineteenth century, the system of Great Public Schools increasingly provided the colleges of Oxford and Cambridge with a dependable clientele. Between 1820 and 1850 a pattern of education emerged at these institutions: emphasis on athletic competition, on loyalty to the school itself, and on the assumption that residence was essential to the educational experience. In addition to these hallmarks, as Sheldon Rothblatt noted, the rules, rituals, and traditions associated with the schools gave them glamour.[24]

The influx of large numbers of public school "old boys" into the universities in the later nineteenth century set a new tone for the sense of community in Oxbridge colleges. Although the notion that living in college was traditionally associated with an Oxford or a Cambridge education, the communal life fostered by the public schools elevated the importance of the residential experience. The increased role of athletics and organized sports was among the most visible manifestations of the public school influence on university life. Games had been a part of the formal curriculum of the public schools since the 1840s, but by the 1860s the "new gospel of athletics" had also taken hold at the universities, and students spent a considerable amount of time on organized sports. Intracollegiate and intercollegiate competition became widespread in a number of team sports, including rowing, cricket, and rugby football. This emphasis on sports intensified the expectation that a university student should be as loyal to his college as he was to be his public school house. Participation typically was compulsory, though that fact was officially denied. And although many observers—both domestic and foreign—admired the importance attached to athletics, a number of English university reformers disliked the importance placed on sports. Many of the men involved in transforming Oxford and Cambridge into modern scholarly institutions realized that athletics often superseded, rather than complemented, academic life.[25]

While Oxbridge tutors were lobbying to establish university teaching as an academic career, the public schools were also helping to redefine the role of the teacher. The clerical don of prereformed Oxford or Cambridge was often perceived as aloof, pedantic, and indifferent. In contrast, beginning with the regime of Thomas Arnold at Rugby in the 1820s, the relationship between teacher and pupil became central to public school education. The master was intended to be the paramount moral and intellectual force in the schoolboy's life. Therefore, the public school old boys brought with them to Oxford and Cambridge the expectation that the relationship between college students and their dons should also be close.[26]

By the late nineteenth century the network of personal associations begun in the public schools were helping Oxford and Cambridge graduates rise to positions of leadership in the British Empire's administrative apparatus. Several residential colleges capitalized on these relationships to create career opportunities for their graduates, thereby making attendance attractive to the largely middle-class constituency who populated the public schools. Thanks to the lobbying of dons, such as Balliol's Benjamin Jowett, and of public servants with Oxbridge ties, university men persuaded the government to orient the educational requirements for civil service positions to contemporary notions of the liberal arts. These efforts resulted in civil service examinations that were based on the curriculum of the English universities.[27]

Besides the advantage the examinations gave to university graduates, the rise of associational networks of public school old boys facilitated preferential treatment within the civil service. Between 1870 and 1920 most public schools established alumni associations, adopted school ties, and published registers. These deliberate efforts to instill school loyalty provided old boys with Oxford and Cambridge degrees a network for social advancement.[28]

In spite of the decisive role played by these associational networks, it became widely held that the success of these men was in fact the result of their university education. As Michael Sanderson observed, "The administration of [government] seemed ample proof that an apparently useless nonvocational form of education did train practical minds who could turn their studies to account for the benefit of their own careers and of society at large. The effectiveness of statesmen like Peel and Gladstone, former Oxford 'intellectuals' of high academic ability, also served to confirm this."[29]

The noumenal past of Oxbridge reveals that historical accident, prevailing political conditions, and social forces within English society helped to shape the character of the two universities. The collegiate university and its curriculum resulted principally from political upheaval and intense reform efforts, not from time-tested educational practice. Indeed, the universities' own reformers were as eager as many Americans to adopt German academic practice and to modernize the courses of study. Likewise, the residential colleges' ability to provide a breeding ground for civic leaders was owed primarily to skillful manipulation of the social network of the public school old boys and not to the content of an Oxbridge education.

The Perceived Past

In contrast to the noumenal past, the popular perception of Oxbridge that emerged in the late nineteenth century often ignored the importance of the many transformations that took place within the universities. It was instead widely asserted that Oxford and Cambridge—which predated the empire, the established church, and even Magna Carta—had molded the character of England's intellectual and political leaders since the Middle Ages. As Sir George R. Parkin, Organizing Secretary of the Rhodes Trust, and graduate of Balliol College, wrote in 1912:

> The great traditions of Oxford are closely connected with an immense range of English history

and of human thought and process. Here Alfred is believed to have organized the beginnings of English academic life; here Roger Bacon started the quest for scientific truth; here William of Wykeham, Wolsey, and others founded centuries ago some of the noblest and still unrivaled educational structures in Europe, worthy homes of learning and religion, to the joint service of which they were dedicated. . . . In these classic walks Addison meditated the Essays which have preserved his fame as a master of English prose; here Samuel Johnson suffered the pains of early poverty and laid the foundations of his prodigious learning. . . . Here Ruskin gave his lectures on Art; here Newman preached the sermons which stirred a generation sunk in indifference to a new spiritual life; here Methodism had its beginning; . . . and here Arnold Toynbee dreamed those dreams of social regeneration founded on social sympathy which have so deeply influenced the thought and effort of our own generation.[30]

Such depictions left little room for academic reformers and dissidents. Indeed, the revolution that transformed late-Victorian Oxbridge was so quiet that many failed to recognize its importance, or even its occurrence. The deadpan treatment of so fundamental a reform, argue Christopher Brooke and Roger Highfield, was characteristically English: "Great changes were carried out through this period because the most enlightened had a blinding vision of what university education could be; because ordinary practical men saw sense and economy in making college lecturers teach; because the most conservative hardly noticed anything was happening."[31]

Given the social tendencies in nineteenth-century England, it was perhaps not surprising that many people felt more comfortable with the past than the present. The past offered imagined security, while the Industrial Revolution and its accompanying social forces were transforming everything familiar. Throughout the nineteenth century, England was rediscovering and reasserting the value of its own cultural heritage. This impulse was perhaps most clearly exemplified by the Gothic Revival of the mid-nineteenth century, which heightened interest in England's most ancient institutions. This movement began in the early 1830s and remained a force in English cultural life for most of the nineteenth century. While most noted for its revitalization of medieval architecture, the Gothic Revival was a full-fledged cultural movement that sought to assert a distinct Anglo-Saxon racial identity. Lord Clark described it as all at once "literary, patriotic, aesthetic and moral."[32]

The Gothic Revival began as a reaction against the prominence of the neoclassical architectural style and the general domination of British cultural life by the tastes of continental Europe. In their efforts to define a cultural ideal that they felt expressed Englishness more authentically, Gothic Revivalists rejected classical antiquity and turned to the late Middle Ages. In the medieval world they saw a coherent and integrated society in which all classes merited equal dignity, craftsmanship was highly valued, and ethics and mysticism coexisted within the framework of a universal church. Although Gothic architecture was prevalent in much of continental Europe as well as in England, the revivalists nevertheless declared the style an embodiment of English national identity. By 1836, Gothic was considered by its adherents to be the only correct and universal form of aesthetic expression.[33]

The most famous exponent of the Gothic Revival was John Ruskin, who expanded on the movement's precepts to make them consistent with mid-nineteenth-century England's imperial vision. To Ruskin, a country's art was "the exponent of its social and political virtues . . . an exact exponent of its ethical life." He believed that he and his countrymen were "rich in an inheritance of honour, bequeathed to us through a thousand years of noble history," and that England had a duty to spread the superiority of Anglo-Saxon culture—and rule—throughout the world.[34]

At the same time that England was growing more conscious of its past, an academic ethos emerged within Oxford and Cambridge based on new ideas of the purposes of education, principally those of John Henry Newman and Matthew Arnold. Newman spent six years as a tutor at Oriel College before his involvement in the Tractarian Movement led to his conversion to Catholicism and his departure from Oxford. In *The Idea of A University* (1852), a collection of sermons delivered while he was rector of the Catholic University of Ireland, Newman rejected the idea that all knowledge should serve an immediate and practical purpose, asserting instead that the object of a higher education was the development of intellect. He argued further that the university was not the proper setting for the creation of philosophical or scientific discovery. He felt that moral education, "beyond that which tended toward the development of intellect," and religious training had no place in the university. He rooted his ideas on education in the tradition of aristocratic civility, but he insisted on intellectual discipline as well. Newman acknowledged that a liberal arts education "does manifest itself in a courtesy, propriety, and polish of word and action, which is beautiful in itself, and acceptable to others; but it does much more. It brings the mind into form—for the mind is like the body. Boys outgrow their shape and their strength; their limbs have to be knit together, and their constitution needs tone."[35]

Newman stressed that the most valuable kind of education was self-education, which prospered in an environment that embraced learning in its totality. In one of the most famous passages of *The Idea of a University*, Newman made his case for the college as an optimal center for intellectual learning. He asserted that a residential environment, in which the students have the opportunity to learn from one another, would be eminently preferable to a university in which there were professorial lectures but nothing else. "That youthful community," argued Newman, "will constitute a whole, it will embody a specific idea, it will represent a doctrine, it will administer a code of conduct, and it will furnish principles of thought and action. It will give birth to a living teaching, which in course of time will take the shape of a self-perpetuating tradition, or a *genius loci*, as it is sometimes called; which haunts the home where it has been born, and . . . forms . . . every individual who is brought under its shadow."[36]

Along with Newman, the most influential exponent of this brand of liberal culture was Thomas Arnold's son Matthew. The younger Arnold spent a great deal of his career as a royal inspector of schools. He became one of Victorian England's most influential educational critics, though he wrote much less than Newman about the specifics of higher education. Deeply concerned with the enormous social changes that occurred in England during his lifetime, Arnold believed that the England of his day, transformed by the forces of democratization and industrialization, was in a condition of spiritual anarchy that in turn made social anarchy more likely. Arnold saw a solution to this condition in the creation of a new elite that was fit to lead not only in the political sense, but intellectually and culturally as well. In his famous essay "Culture and Anarchy" (1868–69) Arnold took issue with contemporary liberal thinking, especially what he considered an overemphasis on individualism and utilitarianism. At the heart of this elite, as Sheldon Rothblatt observed, was Newman's intellectual gentleman, a beau ideal of spiritual balance and moderate temper educated to put his best self forward: "Sustained by the pursuit of perfection, fortified by right reason and the firm intelligible law of things, under no authority but the highest authority, the very idea of authority itself [he] could look out upon the world in calm of mind, all passion spent." Drawing inspiration from the ancient Greek golden mean, Arnold proposed that the educational program for inculcating culture involve the balanced and harmonious expansion of all the powers that enhance the beauty and worth of human nature.[37]

The anti-utilitarianism of Newman's and Arnold's thinking helped to create an impression that the philosophy that governed Oxbridge was slow, evolutionary, and fundamentally conservative. Although they took issue with many of the positions put forward by such men as Edward Copleston, Newman's and Arnold's conception of education had more in common with the earlier generation of conservative thinkers than with their opponents.

The first generation of Oxbridge college histories that were written at the turn of the century also tended to play down the importance of recent reforms in university life. Perhaps because these works were written to instill collegial loyalty and solidarity—a goal that might be undermined by attention to conflict—the histories had a great deal to say about the circumstances surrounding college foundings and famous alumni but little to say about the changes of the previous decades. For example, *Pembroke College, Cambridge: A Short History* (1936) devoted only 13 of 123 pages to the period following 1830. *All Souls College* [Oxford] (1899) dedicated 18 of 226 pages to the nineteenth century. The same period was covered in 17 of 331 pages in *The History of Corpus Christi College* [Oxford] (1893). *Mag-*

dalen College [Oxford] (1899) dedicated about 23 of 264 pages to the nineteenth century.[38]

Even when reformers themselves wrote college histories they often deemphasized the changes. In the *History of Balliol College* (1899), the respected historian H. W. C. Davis devoted only 20 of 200 pages to the nineteenth century. Although he was less apt than other college historians to overvalue the distant past, Davis was nevertheless reluctant to discuss too much of reform-era Balliol, explaining that "it is unnecessary to revive old controversies by discussing in detail each particular innovation through which the College advanced toward her new idea." Again, stressing the importance of continuity rather than departure with the past, Davis insisted that no matter what change took place at Balliol, the ultimate object of all reform was to provide a "liberal education."[39]

Christ's College [Cambridge], published in 1900 by its master, John Peile, provides another example. Peile championed university education for women, fellowship reform, and warm relations between students and dons. Given those credentials, one might have expected him to say much about nineteenth-century college reform at Cambridge. But in his 200-hundred-page-plus volume he devotes scarcely two paragraphs—nestled unobtrusively amid mention of new buildings, lists of fellows, and election of masters—to the creation of teaching posts, fellowship reform, and the fostering of independent research.[40]

This perception of Oxbridge's development was reinforced by the lack of any authoritative history that dealt with the reforms in detail. The first was Charles Edward Mallett's *History of the University of Oxford: Modern Oxford*, published in 1926. Accounts focusing on nineteenth-century reform were still several decades away.[41]

There was a great deal of popular literature that reinforced the notion that major disruptions had not occurred in England's ancient universities. Novels written throughout the nineteenth and well into the twentieth centuries reflected the idea that university life had evolved slowly into its present-day form. Beginning with the publication of *Reginald Dalton: A Story of English University Life,* written by John Gibson Lockhart in 1823, novels about university life, usually set at Oxford, were widely circulated in England and to a lesser degree in America. These novels achieved the status of a genre in the 1850s and '60s, with the appearance of Cuthbert Bede's *Adventures of Verdant Green* and Thomas Hughes' *Tom Brown at Oxford,* the sequel to his popular fictionalized account of public school life, *Tom Brown's Schooldays.* Most of these novels contained a stock plot that emphasized the importance of the social side of college experience, often to the exclusion of most things academic. These novels frequently exaggerated the rowdier aspects of college life, perhaps to deflate the claims of piety made by clerical dons. The university novel remained popular well into the early twentieth century.

Mortimer Proctor has observed that the basic plots of these novels were remarkably uniform. "The freshman, armed with parental advice . . . arrives aboard a coach driven by a cigar-smoking, horn-tooting undergraduate." After arriving at the university and meeting his tutor, the student almost immediately neglects his course of study in favor of more social pastimes, including "vigorous wine parties, a bonfire in the quad, tricks played upon unpopular students, midnight excursions to screw shut the doors of offending tutors, days in the field with hounds and horses and on the river in punt and shell," all of which occupy too much time to allow him to address his studies. "The gay life continues . . . until the awareness of the approaching examination becomes so strong that the scholar locks his door [and] attempts to expiate his sins of omission. When the examination finally arrives, the final cramming pays off, as it is not uncommon for the student to pass with honors. . . . Then, with glory resting heavily upon him, he is ready to enjoy the climax of the college year, when the university is invaded by flocks of fair faces during a week of boat races, college balls, and the ceremonies of awarding degrees."[42]

In the early twentieth century, novelists intensified their emphasis on the interconnectedness of college life and the development of character. Proctor dubbed this new attitude the Cult of Oxford. Plots written in the 1910s and '20s expounded more introspectively about the purpose of a university education. Clearly reflecting the influence of Newman's and Arnold's conception of the development of the beau idéal, novels like Compton Mackenzie's *Sinister Street* (1913) and Beverly Nichols's *Patchwork* (1921) propagated the belief that the most important part of the university experience came from immersing oneself in traditions and culture, eventually coming to understand, like Michael Fane of *Sinister Street,* what the vitality of Oxford's past meant as a "force in the development of man's spirit." The primary educational impact of the college experience sprang from relationships with other Oxonians.[43]

In Transition: Balliol College

The role played by Oxford's Balliol College in the late nineteenth and early twentieth centuries illustrates some of the contradictions between the impact of reform and the perceived importance of tradition. Balliol, one of the oldest of Oxford's colleges, was comparatively small and, for much of its history, relatively poor. In the late nineteenth century, however, Balliol became known for the disproportionate share of eminent men it produced and for its success in placing its graduates in most prestigious branches of government, most notably the India Civil Service.[44]

Balliol's early development was unremarkable in relation to that of other colleges. It was founded in 1255 by John de Balliol, a wealthy landowner of Norman descent. In making an act of contrition following a dispute with the Bishop of Durham, his feudal neighbor, Balliol purchased a house in Oxford that was to serve as a hostel for poor scholars. The college had no statutes, charter, or endowment until 1282, when Balliol's widow, Dervorguilla, became interested in helping the scholars. Two years later she endowed the house with land and bought three adjoining houses. Subsequent endowments increased the size of Balliol, but it remained one of Oxford's poorest and smallest colleges.[45]

Balliol's status did not change until the early nineteenth century, when it became one of the premier institutions of Victorian society. Its rise was the direct result of the prominent positions its masters and tutors played in the reform movements of the era. Two of its masters, Richard Jenkyns and Benjamin Jowett, were involved in the Royal Commissions, and many of their pioneering reforms at Balliol became the basis for the parliamentary mandates of the 1850s and 1870s. Under Jenkyns (1819–54), Balliol opened its scholarships to university-wide competition and its fellowships to those who were not in religious orders. Through Jenkyns' support for scholarship the tutorial corps at Balliol earned a strong reputation within Oxford.[46]

Jowett built on the foundation laid by Jenkyns to bring Balliol to the height of its eminence. Jowett came to Balliol in 1838 as a fellow, became a tutor in 1842, and served as master from 1870 until 1893. He believed in the educational ideals of Matthew Arnold and hoped that Balliol would "make accessible to the world the panacea of which Arnold had already proclaimed." In contrast with the emphasis on routinized classical studies of Copleston's Oxford, Jowett's teaching emphasized self-education and detailed study of the philosophy and literature of ancient Greece. He encouraged friendly intimacy between fellows and undergraduates and advocated the founding of women's colleges. According to A. D. Lindsay, Balliol's master from 1924 to 1949, Jowett "prepared the aristocracy of England to play a real and living part in a democracy . . . and purged them of aristocratic vices."[47]

Jowett understood that connections between the college and the administrative apparatus of the British Empire could be valuable to Balliol's future. He and others successfully lobbied Parliament to reform the examination process for placement in the India Civil Service (ICS), the most prestigious branch of imperial administration, so that university graduates received preferential treatment. The network of old Balliol men within the branches of imperial government, especially the ICS, became self-perpetuating: in the late-Victorian heyday, three successive viceroys of India were Balliol men. Balliol alumni also rose to prominence in other areas of British public life: when Sir Francis Parkin was a Balliol undergraduate in the 1870s, his classmates included future Prime Minister Henry Asquith, future Foreign Secretary Edward Grey, and the journalist St. Loe Strachey, who later became a close friend of Theodore Roosevelt.[48]

Although Balliol gained its prestige by being at the forefront of reform, interpretations of the college's success focused on its distant past. The college boasted a long list of famous alumni, including John Wyclif, suggesting a centuries-old tradition of grooming students for public life. (Although, as Carless Davis observed, two of Balliol's most famous alumni, Adam Smith and Sir William Hamilton, energetically took their alma mater to task for its obsolescence.) The desire to connect Balliol more closely to its medieval past was literally set in stone. In 1802 the exterior of the college's quadrangle, which dated to the four-teenth century, had been given a neoclassical face-lift, reflecting the architectural preferences of the time. In the 1860s the quadrangle was remodeled again, this time in the Gothic Revival style. The new exterior was, however, far more ornate than the original Gothic edifice.[49]

James Leigh Strachan-Davidson, Balliol's master from 1907 to 1916, personified this odd mix of reform and reverence for the past. In the aftermath of the sweeping reform that culminated under Jowett, Strachan set a tone for Balliol that steadfastly, if somewhat ironically, adhered to the perceived notions of Oxford tradition. Unlike earlier masters, Strachan was not a minister, but he comported himself with a monastic devotion to the college that equaled that of his clerical predecessors. Although the scholarly reputation of a college relied increasingly on married, nonresidential dons, Strachan was contemptuous of the exercise of such prerogatives, openly chiding men who "committed matrimony." He successfully opposed student initiatives to shorten weekday prayer and often gave the first readings in those services himself.[50]

Nevertheless, Strachan understood the contemporary sources of Balliol's strength. Although he espoused the clerical lifestyle for college dons, he did not hinder the maintenance of high scholarship in the college. He maintained the tight relationship with the colonial civil services established under Jowett and devoted considerable effort to recruiting students from the Great Public Schools. Those students accounted for two-thirds of Balliol's enrollment in the early 1900s. Consistent with the self-perception of his college and university, the capstone of Strachan's eulogy was not his promotion of scholarship or his acumen in maintaining Balliol's niche in the machinery of the empire. Instead, Strachan's students reflected that "we just had the feeling that he was the greatest gentleman we have ever known."[51]

At the beginning of the twentieth century, Oxford and Cambridge were paradoxical institutions. They were touted to be venerable, evolving slowly toward an ultimate ideal state. But little of what went on at Oxford and Cambridge at the turn of the century was as old as Merton College's Mob Quad or the old court of Corpus Christi College. The changes that took place in Victorian Oxbridge were as revolutionary as the changes occurring in colleges and universities in the United States. The old university of clerics living on fellowships had been replaced by a cadre of academic scholars who, thanks to far-reaching reforms, could now hope to make a career out of their calling. College life, once exemplified by indifference to both scholarship and students, had been only recently reformed by an ethos, largely imported from the public schools, that held the college to be a surrogate family. Both Englishmen and foreigners alike missed much of the significance of these changes. Although careful examiners might see that strong tension existed between notions of gentlemanliness and efforts to forge English seats of modern scholarship, most observers assumed that Arnold's golden mean of cultural, intellectual, and physical perfection had been handed down from generation to generation at Oxbridge.

2

The Whole Man
and the Gentleman Scholar

While "quiet" revolutions occurred at Oxford and Cambridge, many of the leading institutions of higher education in the United States underwent visible transformation between 1860 and 1910. Although considerable cross-pollenization of educational ideas among England, France, and the United States took place during this period, the German university exerted the strongest influence on the development of colleges and universities. The academic ethos of the university—the creation and advancement of knowledge—was first widely accepted in Germany. By 1910 it had taken hold at several well-known American universities. The collegial notions of mental discipline and piety gave way to curricula geared toward creating specialists in individual fields of advanced knowledge.[1]

The importation of research scholarship was not greeted with enthusiasm by everyone in American academe. An outnumbered but vociferous group of educators in several research-oriented universities expressed strong dissatisfaction with the way that the new emphasis on research detracted from undergraduate education. These critics—who included Princeton University President Woodrow Wilson (1902–10) and Harvard President Abbot Lawrence Lowell (1909–33)—found natural allies in the leaders of small colleges. In spite of their disaffection with the prevailing state of affairs, the dissidents did not advocate the commitment to piety and mental discipline espoused by the older generation of classicists. Instead, they turned to the idea of "educating the whole man" as a new expression of their purpose and as a reaction against a society that was becoming dominated by corporate ideas and values. As Frederick Rudolph observed, the whole man "became a symbol that represented values that were conservative, anti-progressive, elitist and non materialistic."[2]

The proponents of educating the whole man asserted that the value of an undergraduate education did not lie in the mastery of a discrete body of knowledge, although they clearly favored the humanities. Rather, they agreed with Wilson that the college ought to cultivate the student's intellectual and spiritual life. "What we should seek to impart in our colleges," Wilson maintained, "is not so much learning, but the spirit of learning." In this vein, they saw the totality of college life, not just the classroom, as an instrument of personal development. Extracurricular contact between student and teacher should play as important a role as formal instruction in the educational process. Instructors ought to share the benefits of their life experience with their students as well as contribute to scholarship in their disciplines. With these purposes in mind, the college experience should ensconce students in what Wilson described as a "garden of the mind."[3]

The notion of educating the whole man was more potent as a symbol that drew on the perceived virtues of the past—and as a reaction against current developments—than as a forward-looking statement on the purposes of higher education. It possessed no coherent curricular strategy, and, indeed, its proponents did not always agree on how to accomplish their educational purposes. As Laurence Veysey noted, "the challenging task . . . was to implant the essence of a 2,500-year-old civilization into the minds of youthful Americans, each of whom could be reached only in large groups allotted a mere three hours per week. As to the need for such a task, the members of the academic faction were solidly in agreement. As to its practicability, however, they were divided, frequently in their own minds."[4]

Two developments in contemporary university life were deemed particularly adverse to the development of the whole person. Not surprisingly, both were linked to the German university's influence on American higher education. The first of these was the free elective system, introduced at Harvard University during the presidency of Charles W. Eliot (1869–1909). Redolent of German university *Lernfreiheit*, the elective system allowed students considerable freedom in choosing among academic course offerings. Many opponents argued that this created an academic marketplace in which an underinformed consumer—the student—had to make major decisions about his program on his own. Both Wilson and Lowell, who followed Eliot as Harvard president, felt strongly that students could acquire a broadened intellectual outlook only if the course of study proceeded in a coherent and orderly fashion. According to Lowell, the ideal college education provided a general understanding of a number of specified areas of study and a thorough mastery of one.[5] This objective might not be attainable under a system that allowed students to choose their own courses and to take them in any sequence they desired. The undergraduate curriculum therefore required some measure of prescription to ensure that students received a balanced education that followed a logical plan.

Their second concern was that the university might abandon its role in the noncurricular lives of students. In the 1860s the University of Michigan abolished student dormitories, and two decades later Harvard discontinued mandatory residence on campus. However, the reasons that these and other universities chose to discontinue, or at least deemphasize, housing students in supervised dormitories was not solely an imitation of German practice, in which students were expected to fend for themselves. Dormitories were expensive to build and maintain, and money was often needed for other projects. Many campuses, particularly in the Midwest and South, grew to depend on Greek-letter societies to provide organized housing for students. Lowell and other educators felt that the residential experience was an integral part of undergraduate education and that curriculum alone could not direct the development of students' character. The journalist John Corbin voiced similar sentiment in a series of essays on American universities he wrote for the *Saturday Evening Post* in 1908. Corbin argued that in most American universities "the crying need is of a better ordered residential life. The influences that make most strongly for character and culture are not those which adorn moments of social leisure, but those which operate without intermission in the normal and inevitable occupations — eating and sleeping, work and play."[6]

These men did not need to look far for evidence to reinforce their opinions about student culture. Students of the time appeared to spend considerable time unsupervised by faculty, prompting Wilson to declare that extracurricular activities had become the "sideshow that had swallowed the circus." Instead of an extracurriculum that drew faculty members and students into informal but intellectual colloquy, students inhabited a world that reflected their own sense of order and that seemed to bear out Wilson's concern over the creation of "two separate air-tight compartments in [students'] consciousness." Edwin Slosson, who wrote a series of essays on American universities that appeared in *The Observer* in 1909 and 1910, agreed on this point. He called the diversion of the student body's interest from the "true aims of the college" the greatest problem American universities had to face.[7]

Fraternities and athletics were considered the primary sources of student distraction. Although many observers ac-

knowledged that fraternities provided a homelike and structured atmo sphere, they were nevertheless seen as engines that
drove students' interests away from intellectual concerns. The
relation between fraternity and academy could vary greatly from
institution to institution; Corbin had mixed reactions to the
fraternities he visited at the University of Michigan but thought
that life in Wisconsin's chapters was "agreeable and profitable."
At some schools, a cordial relation existed between the fraternity system and host institution, while at others, like Princeton, faculty worked fervently to rid their school of Greek-letter
chapters.[8]

Intercollegiate athletic competition, usually in the form of
football, was the most visible of the "sideshows." In the late
nineteenth century, football was the most popular student activity, even though few students actually played the game. The
enjoyment of following the school team commanded students'
attention, and the "big game" was a focus of campus social activities. Although many college administrators clearly appreciated the attention that successful teams brought to their institutions, they were dismayed that following the college team—
and not the curriculum—had become the experience that affirmed one's association with his school.[9]

To some observers, sports were being accorded far too much
attention, preventing the development of balanced individuals.
Few critics, however, were willing to consider that the popularity of college athletics might have more to do with changes
in the overall fabric of society than with the insular world of
the college. Perhaps unaware of the increasing role that spectator sports were playing in American life in the Progressive
Era, Lowell blamed the rise of athletics on faculty indifference
toward students and suggested that better student-faculty relations might remedy the situation.[10]

Although they saw themselves as dissenters from the con

temporary conception of a university, Wilson, Lowell, and those who sympathized with them felt that the weight of educational tradition was on their side. They firmly believed that a close personal relationship between student and teacher had existed in the old-time college but had been undone by the indifference of German-trained research scholars to the personal development of students. Moreover, they saw curricular fragmentation and the deluge of extracurricular activities as evidence of how the germanized research scholar had undermined the moral character of American undergraduate education. Wilson argued that "we have now for a long generation devoted ourselves to promoting changes which have resulted in all but complete disorganization." And W. H. Cowley, president of Hamilton College in Clinton, New York, and an admirer of Wilson, reflected a few years later that the new breed of research scholar had "undermined the 'collegiate way of living.' "[11]

A popular quotation of the Progressive Era held that the ideal teaching arrangement was "[Williams College President] Mark Hopkins on one end of the log, and a student on the other." The nostalgic appeal of this image was used on more than one occasion to suggest that contact between student and teacher, the elemental component of any education, was missing in the American university classroom. Slosson blamed this lack of personal contact on the germanized research scholars, whom he characterized as a "new school of teachers, who detest teaching, who look upon students as a nuisance and classwork as a waste of time." Slosson felt that every college student should have "at least one friend in the faculty, some one [*sic*] who knows his training and home conditions, his mode of life and ways of working, his aims and prospects, his capabilities and deficiencies." However compelling his language, Slosson, like other critics of germanization, were overshadowed by those who saw original investigation and usefulness to the greater society as the primary emphases for the university.[12]

Given the characteristics that the American "whole man" shared with his English counterpart, the gentleman scholar, it is not surprising that many of the critics of the germanized university found a compelling source of inspiration in contemporary England. Beginning in the late 1890s, Cambridge and especially Oxford were regularly looked to as exemplars of an arrangement in which scholars and students shared a close relationship. Several features of the English pattern of higher education appeared to address the deficiencies of the contemporary American university. First, Americans admired the way that Oxbridge students lived, along with many of their teachers, in the residential colleges. This system of organizing the university around bodies of students and teachers rather than bodies of knowledge was perhaps the fundamental distinction between Oxbridge and American universities. The residential colleges were small autonomous communities that commanded the primary loyalty of their students—that is, a student was a King's man or a Balliol man first and an Oxonian second. The college's organizational pattern, its human scale, and the opportunity it provided for interaction among students were credited with shaping the students' social and intellectual development. The educational value of the residential colleges looked particularly appealing to Charles Thwing, president of Western Reserve University, who wrote in 1911 that the "talk of the common room, the intimacies of the breakfast and luncheon, the pulling of oars of the same boat, constant and intimate associations represent forces and conditions which help to make men."[13]

Within the college, the English undergraduate received individualized instruction from a tutor, who met regularly with the student. Each student was required to compose essays on his current readings that would be critiqued at each session. Outside the tutorial, students and teachers had many opportunities to meet and interact on a less formal basis, although colleges generally maintained a fairly rigid separation between student and teacher, including separate common rooms and separate dining tables. The student had to pass a comprehensive examination in his chosen area of study before a degree was granted. While the American student was tested for each course credit, the English college man underwent only two comprehensive examinations during his college career, the second of which led to the bachelor's degree. The system of pass and honours degrees created different tracks, depending on the level of academic specialization sought.

The most visible manifestation of the perceived superiority of this system was its product: the Oxford or Cambridge man himself, who displayed social and intellectual skills far beyond those of the typical American undergraduate. "Our American boys," wrote James Anderson Hawes, Delta Kappa Epsilon general secretary, "are unable to discuss politics, they are ignorant of the latest plays and of literature, have a very limited power of expression when describing what they saw or did when traveling abroad and cannot even frankly compare or discuss college affairs beyond athletics and one or two other topics." Conversely, the exemplary Oxonian or Cantabridgian was at ease in social gatherings, well read, well spoken, and dedicated to assuming a position of leadership in his nation's service. "The colleges," wrote W. H. Cowley, "have supplied the empire with men at once splendidly and admirably cultivated socially. Without labeling oneself Anglophile, one can assent with assurance that Oxford and Cambridge have come nearer to satisfying the scholar-and-gentleman ideal than the universities of any other nation." And the academic reputation of Oxbridge students was strong. "A well educated Englishman," Lowell recounted, "is said to be one who has forgotten Greek." [14]

Occasional support for the idea of importing the English residential college system even came from proponents of the research ideal. Daniel Coit Gilman, president of Johns Hopkins, showed interest in the idea but was not ready to blame the condition of undergraduate education on his fellow Germanized scholars. Gilman did agree that residence had an important role to play in education, but he blamed the shabby condition of many college dormitories for the low regard for residential education. Nevertheless, he hoped that the example of Oxford and Cambridge would spur interest in residential undergraduate education. "One experiment remains to be tried," he asserted in 1893, citing the "establishment of a hall of residence which shall be to the university what a college is to Oxford and Cambridge, a hotel, with a scholar and staff at the head of it; with privacy, comfort, oversight and intellectual guidance." [15]

The tendency for American elites to look to England for cultural and social direction reinforced the notion that American universities might well improve themselves by adopting features of Oxford and Cambridge. Throughout the nineteenth and into the twentieth centuries England was an important point of reference on pressing social questions.[16] Besides sharing a common body of literary tradition, there was considerable contact between educators on both sides of the Atlantic. Although Americans and Englishmen differed on a number of educational issues, American school reformers generally looked to England for theories and models.[17]

German-trained research scholars might have had the greatest influence on late-nineteenth-century American universities, but the general tone of American literary and intellectual life was still connected closely to England. The way that Americans viewed England was fundamentally different from the way they tended to view other countries. That view was rooted in what Henry Steele Commager called a "special relationship" that differed "not only in degree but even in kind from those with other nations." Americans who traveled to continental Europe did so largely to study and become conversant in the country's educational strengths; such was the case with prospective scholars in the sciences going to Germany and future architects attending the Ecole de Beaux-Arts in France. But while some Americans traveled to England "on business," Commager explained, "the majority . . . who visited and wrote about [England] did so to satisfy themselves about the character of the Mother Country, and about their own relationship to her." As Edward Shils noted, in the eyes of American visitors England "acquired a topography almost like that of the Holy Land."[18]

The close cultural relation between England and America was reflected strongly in the countries' literary relation. As Commager observed, Americans and the English knew each other from early childhood. Americans read *Mother Goose* and *Alice in Wonderland, Tom Brown's Schooldays* and *The Jungle Book;* their English counterparts read *Little Women* and *Tom Sawyer.* They shared each other's heroes and villains. "Every English schoolboy," observed Commager, "had read Thackeray's moving tribute to George Washington in *The Virginians* and many of them knew 'by heart,' as Churchill did, 'The Midnight Ride of Paul Revere,' . . . [and] almost every American schoolboy had read Macaulay's essay on Clive and could recite at least some lines of 'The Charge of the Light Brigade.'"[19]

Beyond a sense of literary commonality, the special relationship furnished the United States with an ancestry that extended its history much further back in time. This was an especially agreeable association for American colleges and universities, because Oxford and Cambridge were among the oldest of all English institutions. "So far as noble and historic traditions can give inspiration," Sir Charles Parkin noted, "Oxford stands almost unique among English centres of life." These sentiments were echoed in America by Charles Franklin Thwing, who called Oxford simply "the best of England raised to its highest power."[20]

Since the 1890s, Britain and the United States had become close allies and trading partners, links that went beyond simple alignment of political interests. Like Woodrow Wilson, who was to become his political rival in 1912, President Theodore Roosevelt was an ardent Anglophile. During his career Roosevelt spent a considerable amount of time visiting England and cultivating relationships with politically influential figures. He and his British associates believed that the ascendancy of the United States and the British Empire rose from a common heritage of language and civic institutions. As Sir George Clark wrote in the English periodical *Nineteenth Century*, "The same forces that have created the British Empire have built the great republic." In a similar vein, Roosevelt's close friend St. Loe Strachey wrote in *The Spectator*, another English magazine, that Britain and the United States shared a "sympathy of comprehension" that made the states natural allies.[21]

Three sources of English influence in particular fueled Anglophile tendencies in American academic culture. First, the Gothic Revival spread from England to the United States in the 1870s, intensifying the feeling of common racial identity with England within an influential minority and resulting in the proliferation of Gothic architecture on American campuses. Second, a body of popular literature by American and English writers proclaimed the advantages of the English pattern of higher education. Finally, the establishment of the Rhodes Scholarships in 1902 brought into American higher educational establishment a number of men cultivated to be advocates of English society.

It was perhaps ironic that the new interest in English civil and educational institutions came just as the American national identity was becoming less enmeshed with British culture. A new sense of Americanism accompanied the transformation of the United States into a leading corporate and industrial state during the post–Civil War years and Progressive Era. Commager explained that as America began to take its own pre-eminence for granted, interest in "identity" became less dependent on English culture: "The twentieth century American concluded the American character was not to be sought in the corridors of English history, but rather in the experiences and conditions of American life."[22]

As this new American self-image grew, Gothic Revivalism took hold within a limited but influential sector of American society. By the 1880s the Gothic Revival movement was running out of steam in Britain but becoming popular with a circle of architects and academics in the United States. Although the idealization of the Middle Ages probably enjoyed limited serious consideration in America, the rhetoric of Anglo-Saxon racial superiority found adherents among elites concerned with the changes occurring American society. The influx of non-English-speaking, non-Protestant immigrants from southern and eastern Europe was condemned for its supposedly deleterious effect on American society. As a belief system, Anglo-Saxon racial superiority was compatible with the precepts of eugenics and Social Darwinism.

In the eyes of architect Ralph Adams Cram, the Revival's most fervent American spokesman, Gothic style became a metaphor for a culture under siege. In contrast with the materialism he saw in contemporary society, Gothic was a "symbol of high truth and fine ideals ardently and bravely pursued; of a oneness of life that extends into every category of thought and action and involves all classes of men; a symbol of the best at any time, of spiritual truths recognized and sought and in some sense achieved." To Cram, the great task before himself and other civic and cultural leaders was to build a "new society that will make inevitable, by its nobility, art that shall speak again to history of the beauty and the righteousness of the life that brings it to being."[23]

This characterization of the Gothic Revival reflected differences in the mindsets and concerns of adherents on both sides of the Atlantic. Ruskin's rhetoric ultimately led to a sense of imperial transcendence; Cram's words reflected the social pressures that American elites faced in a world where deference to old values appeared to be slipping away.

College campuses provided the most visible evidence of the Gothic Revival in America. Beginning with plans for Trinity College in Hartford, Connecticut, in 1870 (less than a decade after Balliol's face-lift), Gothic designs gained popularity in college and university building projects, even though the most influential architectural style of the period was associated with the Ecole de Beaux-Arts. Cram, for one, saw his role as an architect of higher education as facilitating the transmission of English cultural heritage: "My business is to . . . pick up the old traditions of college architecture that belongs to our [Anglo-Saxon] race and to adopt those forms, so recovered, to whatever conditions may have come into being."[24] He noted further that the adoption of Gothic architecture reflected the intention of American colleges and universities to set their English heritage in stone: "When again we try to restore to our colleges, as at Princeton and the University of Pennsylvania and Chicago and Bryn Mawr, something of the wonderful dynamic architecture of Oxford and Cambridge and Eton and Winchester, we do it far less because we like the style better than that—or rather those—of Columbia and Harvard and Yale, than because we are impelled to our course by an instinctive mental affiliation with the cultural impulses behind the older art and with the cultural and educational principles for which they stand."[25]

At Princeton University, more than the style of the building was important in reflecting an Anglo-Saxon heritage. As supervising architect, Cram executed an asymmetric building plan that gave the appearance of a community that, like Oxford and Cambridge, had grown organically over the centuries. When Wilson visited Cambridge in 1899 he described it in terms that suggested his conception of a garden of the mind: "a place full of quiet chambers, secluded ancient courts, and gardens shut away from intrusion—a town full of coverts, for those who would learn and be with their own thoughts." In 1910, Andrew West, dean of Princeton Graduate School, described Princeton in language that evoked the same images: "quadrangles shadowing sunny lawns, towers and gateways opening into quiet retreats, ivy-grown walls looking on sheltered gardens . . . these are the places where the affections linger and where memories cling like the ivies themselves, and these are the answers in architecture and scenic setting to the immemorial longings of Academic generations." Although his choice of language was simpler, Wilson was pleased with the new power of suggestion that his campus held. He contended that "by the very simple device of building our new buildings in the Tudor Gothic Style we seem to have added to Princeton the age of Oxford and Cambridge; we have added a thousand years to the history of Princeton by merely putting those lines in our buildings which point every man's attention to the historical traditions of learning in the English-speaking race."[26]

By 1930 many of America's most well-known colleges and universities had taken on a decidedly Gothic appearance. Besides Princeton's almost complete transformation, Yale's Harkness Quadrangle (1917), designed by James Gamble Rogers, and Cope and Stewardson's dormitories at the University of Pennsylvania (1895) became the architectural foci of their campuses. Some alumni had mixed feelings about the transformations, but Henry Seidel Canby wrote that he felt a sense of reserved pride in Yale, his newly ancient alma mater. He observed that the alumni welcomed enthusiastically the "final triumph of the Gothic scheme which at frightful expense transformed the ugly college into a new Oxford, equipped not like the original for monastic students, but with every appurtenance of the life of the very rich, and housed in the ornate plush-in-stone of the late Middle Ages which gave a striking effect of class exclusiveness. I write not entirely in sorrow, for the college was vital, and deserved to be dressed in fine linen and set upon a throne."[27]

At the same time that interest in the architecture of medieval Oxbridge became popular, literature about life in the English universities found its way to America. In addition to the Oxford novels, articles on Oxford and Cambridge appeared frequently in popular magazines, sometimes to correct misinterpretations propagated by the novels. The authors generally supported the notion that an Oxford or a Cambridge education imparted social and intellectual skills far superior to what could be learned at American universities.

One of the earliest accounts of English university life by an American was Charles Astor Bristed's *Five Years in an English University*, which appeared in 1852. After studying at Yale, Bristed went to Trinity College, Cambridge, and became one of the few Americans of his time to obtain a degree from an English university. His book first appeared as a series of magazine sketches, but Bristed felt strongly that a more comprehensive work was needed to provide Americans with an accurate depiction of English university life that would counter the images evoked by novels like *Verdant Green*.[28] Although Bristed described at length the rigors of his own classical education, he devoted ample attention to the way that activities such as wine parties and boat races rounded out his educational experience.

The nonfiction literature of four decades later reflected a

changed state of affairs on both sides of the Atlantic. In 1894, George Birkbeck Norman Hill, the editor of Boswell's *Life of Johnson*, spent two months in residence at Harvard University. Afterward, he wrote *Harvard by an Oxonian*, in which he compared the English and American patterns of higher education and spoke in terms that were largely sympathetic to the views of Lowell and Wilson. In short, he admired Harvard for its scholarship, but he felt that it lacked the sense of community and home that Oxford provided its students: "How happy would a University be," Hill wrote, "[that] combined the social life and the friendly intercourse of thought and knowledge which are found in every one of our Oxford Colleges. Each one of them is a gathering-place, the home, of a small knot of learned men. Each of the Common-Rooms is a centre of kindly feeling and hospitality. Of these things we have twenty—Harvard has not one." He also stressed the key role that social interaction played in preserving continuity with the past. An English university education allowed the student to live amid "great floating traditions of learning and mental refinement handed down from distant centuries."[29]

Perhaps the most widely read proponent of anglicizing the American university was John Corbin. A Harvard graduate, Corbin spent 1894–95 at Balliol College, and afterward he joined the editorial staff of Harper and Brothers in New York. Over the course of his career he wore many literary hats, including that of journalist, drama critic for the *New York Times*, and amateur historian. Besides his previously mentioned works, Corbin wrote essays on English and American school life for several popular magazines, including the *Saturday Evening Post*, *Harper's Weekly* and the *Atlantic Monthly*. In 1902, *An American At Oxford* appeared, a popular collection of Corbin's essays on English collegiate life. Like Bristed, Corbin attempted to counter public misconceptions about Oxford. In contrast with his often critical opinion of American college and university life, and, echoing Arnold's Hellenism, Corbin presented Oxford as an institution that integrated harmoniously the intellectual, social, and athletic pursuits of its students. Corbin also asserted that what made Oxford a truly great university was that its practices embodied centuries-old intellectual and social traditions that he contended typified "centuries of the best of English life."[30]

Like Lowell, Corbin believed that the teutonized faculty had wrought social chaos on the American college and that a solution lay in adopting some of the Oxbridge pattern: "Our American universities do not now afford, or are they likely to afford, [a coherent education] until the social and educational systems are more perfectly organized than they have ever been, or seem likely to be, under the dominance of German ideals. . . . We have assimilated or are assimilating the best spirit of German education; and if we make a similar draft on the best educational spirit of England, our universities will become far superior as regards their organization and ideals." Mirroring further the concerns of Wilson and Lowell, Corbin illustrated how the English system addressed the problems of curricular incoherence and the indifference of students to intellectual concerns. In so doing, however, he oversimplified differences between the English and American systems. "In America," Corbin wrote, "the election of studies goes by fragmentary subjects, and the degree is awarded for passing some four subjects a year, the whole number being as disconnected, even chaotic, as the student pleases or as chance decrees." In contrast, Corbin asserted that in England the "degree is granted for final proficiency in a well balanced course of study; but within this not unreasonable limit there is utmost freedom of election." This explanation underplayed the specialized nature of English undergraduate study.[31]

Corbin devoted much of *An American at Oxford* to describing the social and recreational life of the Oxford undergraduate, which he believed to be superior to what existed in American institutions of higher education. Like many Englishmen, he was convinced that athletics played a prominent role in an Oxonian's regimen without succumbing to the element of professionalism in American collegiate sports. He observed that the network of residential colleges facilitated greater participation in sports, because each college fielded its own teams and crews, and because most competition occurred within the university community. And, unlike American collegiate sportsmen, whom Corbin viewed as too concerned with winning, Oxonians appeared to relish sport primarily for personal enjoyment and satisfaction. Nowhere was the contrast between English and American priorities greater than on the football field, where the differences in national personalities had resulted in two very different games: English rugby and American gridiron football. To Corbin, this development became a metaphor for the difference between the balanced ideal of English civility and the specialization that had so permeated Progressive Era America: "The Englishman," Corbin argued, "has on the whole subordinated the elements of skill in combination to the pleasantness of the sport, while the American has somewhat sacrificed the playability of the game to his insatiate struggle for success and his inexhaustible ingenuity for achieving it." [32]

Corbin argued that American institutions of higher education could improve the quality of their undergraduate instruction if they adopted features of the Oxford pattern. He called attention to an 1894 *Harvard Graduate's Magazine* article by Frank Bolles, the late secretary of the Harvard Board of Overseers. Bolles believed that the expanding size of the student body, combined with the increasing specialization of university administrative officers, was destroying much of the personal knowledge that had once existed between deans and students. As an alternative, Bolles suggested dividing the undergraduate student body into more manageable groups, each under the supervision of its own dean. Corbin expanded on Bolles' prescription by suggesting that an adapted form of the English residential college serve the purpose. He proposed that the American colleges and universities subdivide into smaller units, or halls, which would reproduce the intimacy and intellectual environment of the Oxford college.[33]

Like Cram and the Gothicists, Corbin believed that the roots of American higher education lay in the English universities of the Middle Ages. He contended that until the 1860s, when German influence began to assert itself, the constitutions of American universities were similar to those of the Oxbridge colleges. On this basis he proposed that if American universities reembraced the idea of student residence following Oxford's model, the result would equal the most well-developed higher educational system of the Middle Ages, which he thought was the apex of institutional development. Corbin's exaltation of the medieval university was complemented by his belief that the American character, though now distinct from the English, still possessed latent Anglo-Saxon tendencies that might emerge if given succor. While he noted that the "purpose and result of adopting English methods was not to imitate foreign custom," he nevertheless felt that "if the American educational ideals in the end approximate the English more closely than they do at present, such a result would be merely incidental to the fact that the two countries have at bottom much the same social character and instincts."[34]

Corbin's hopes for closer relations between Oxford and American universities were echoed by Englishmen. In 1895, when George Birkbeck Hill visited Harvard, he expressed his hope that the flow of American students to Germany might someday be diverted to England. He looked forward to the day when the "graduate of Harvard and Yale . . . shall wear the gown in the colleges of Oxford and Cambridge, and tread the cloisters which were trodden by their forefathers."[35]

Although Hill could only regret the lack of close ties between Oxford and America, his countryman Cecil Rhodes was in a position to do far more than simply dream of the future. Rhodes, who had heard Ruskin lecture at Oxford while a student at Oriel College in the 1870s, had gone on to amass an enormous fortune in South Africa's diamond industry. Moved by Ruskin's conviction that the Anglo-Saxons owed it to the world to serve as custodians of order and civilization, Rhodes dedicated himself to uniting English-speakers worldwide. Early in his life Rhodes expressed a desire to see the United States reintegrated into the British Empire, but in his mature vision he sought ways to facilitate closer relations between the "two great branches of the Anglo-Saxon family." In spite of these sentiments, however, there was little in the way of scholarly activity that might draw the serious student to choose an English university over a German or an American one. The absence of specialized programs reinforced a general perception in America that Oxford and Cambridge did not value intellectual achievements.[36]

This situation changed decisively in 1902 when Rhodes' bequest established a number of scholarships enabling college graduates from English-speaking nations to study at Oxford. Rhodes saw the Oxford experience as a way to help develop men who could advance his cause after his death. Reflecting the Victorian conception of a scholar-statesman, Rhodes was not looking for students whose primary interest lay in specialized study. He instead hoped to recruit "those who have shown during their school days that they have the instincts to lead" and "to esteem the performance of public duties as their highest aim." Academic promise was to be only one of many traits they needed to possess, and Rhodes was pointedly opposed to bookworms. Twenty percent of the selection criteria was to be based on "participation of a manly sport."[37]

In America, reaction to the idea was positive. William Torrey Harris, the U.S. commissioner of education, applauded the announcement of the bequest. He asserted that Oxford's elevated social atmosphere would "afford the best preliminary training for the experts required in [American] consulates, embassies, home cabinets and international commissions." Only a few detractors worried that Oxford might taint American scholars' virtues. A 1902 editorialist in the *Boston Evening Transcript* expressed his concern that "Rhodes Scholars would be rendered untrue to democratic ideals by associating with Lords wearing gold tassels."[38] The feeling of the commonality of English-speaking peoples expressed by Harris reflected the public mood more accurately: "Our American students need have no fear that they will lose their nationality at Oxford; for they will find the English ideal of a gentleman exactly fitted for Anglo-Saxons everywhere."[39]

Whether one embraced or suspected Rhodes' intentions, the question of how closely the scholars would keep America aligned with England proved moot: the majority of American Rhodes Scholars did not form themselves into a cadre of scholar-statesmen. Between 1903 and 1946, only 7 percent of the 1,123 American Rhodes Scholars entered government service. During the same time, however, the Rhodes Scholarships did make a significant impact on American academe. More than 39 percent of the American Rhodes Scholars became educators, mostly at universities.[40] For the first time since the colonial era the American higher education system was infused with individuals intimately familiar with the English collegial pattern of education. But instead of becoming public advocates of the English system, as Rhodes had envisioned, many of the Rhodes Scholars instead urged that English patterns be adapted to American universities. Among the Rhodes Scholars who promoted tutorial education, comprehensive exams, and an increased emphasis on the residential experience were Pomona College President E. Wilson Lyon, St. John's College reformers Stringfellow Barr and Scott Buchanan, and Swarthmore College President Frank Aydelotte. Between 1902 and 1946, thirteen Rhodes Scholars became presidents of colleges or universities.[41]

Aydelotte, one of the first Rhodes Scholars, was one of the most fervent advocates of importing Oxford practice to America. During his presidency of Swarthmore College (1921–40) he instituted an honors curriculum modeled after Oxford's degree system. In 1910, while a professor of English at Indiana University, he wrote a series of essays that extolled Oxford, and he set forth explicitly the Oxonian gentleman-scholar as the model for the wholly educated man. Like Corbin, Aydelotte wrote from his experience as a student in both English and American universities. He described Oxford in a way that made its salient features readily understandable to Americans with no prior knowledge of English higher education: "It is impossible to understand the cheerful, hospitable home-like life of the Oxford college without some understanding of the Oxford college system. The colleges bear the same relation to the university that our states do to the Nation. . . The college is a sort of enlarged American fraternity, heavily endowed, engaging in the business of instruction and discipline, determining the life of the undergraduate in all its human and social aspects."[42]

In his first essay, "The Oxford Stamp," which appeared in the *North American Student* in June and November 1916, Aydelotte argued that there were three hallmarks of an Oxford education. First, he claimed that the residential college, as it existed in

England, gave invaluable education through good conversation, which occurred at meals and at other social occasions. Second, he endorsed participation in athletics for all students, not just those with outstanding physical talent, to provide training in sportsmanship. Third, he advocated a system of teaching that stressed the student's responsibility for educating himself.[43]

Aydelotte felt that American universities undervalued social intercourse as an educational experience—considering it a waste of time, even—so he took time to explain its role in the development of character. Under favorable conditions, such as those that existed in English residential colleges, social time could be one of the most valuable aspects of the collegiate experience, he argued. To Aydelotte, social life offered Oxford men "an opportunity of acquiring. . . an openness and alertness of mind, a certain independence in thinking, and a readiness, which is almost impossible to acquire in any other way."[44]

Aydelotte's writings also indicated that he shared some of Rhodes' vision of a world run by English-speaking peoples. He saw the Rhodes Scholars as playing an important role in maintaining the bond between the United States and Britain and thereby fulfilling their destiny to maintain peace and order in the world. In "A Challenge to Rhodes Scholars," printed in *American Oxonian* in January 1917, he wrote that "for the first time in history the Anglo-Saxon nations of the world are united. Their union has been brought about not so much by the desires of idealists to lay a foundation for world peace, as by the stupid blunders of a common foe. It will depend on quieter and more intelligent forces to ensure that after the war this union will be continued, will become some kind of league to enforce for all times the rights of smaller states, and to uphold the cause of justice and peace between larger ones."[45]

Aydelotte and other former Rhodes men often drew on the writings of Matthew Arnold and Cardinal Newman to accentuate their praise of Oxford. From their writings a picture of the English university emerged that suggested ways to remedy deficiencies in undergraduate education. Out of these influences, two themes appeared consistently. First, English universities had a pedagogical system that could be adapted to American needs and thereby produce men who were intellectually and socially well rounded. This balance might then correct the problems wrought by academic specialization and the Teutonic research scholars. Second, forging a closer connection to Oxford and Cambridge presumably would raise America's consciousness of its Anglo-Saxon common culture and expand the bond of sympathy with the "mother country." The British Empire and the United States together would assume a critical role in shaping the world's future.

The views of Robert P. Tristam Coffin typified the feelings of many Rhodes Scholars who entered American academic life after leaving England. In an article in *The Forum* in 1923, Coffin described an Oxford education as a lesson in the moderation of all pursuits, a living model of Arnold's thoughts on the cultivation of a cultural elite. "Whatever else the University might teach," Coffin wrote, "she schools [the undergraduate] in the way to enjoy himself, here and now, while the bloom of his prime is still upon him. He can work, play or find the golden mean in all things."[46]

For their part, the English generally welcomed the Rhodes Scholars but noted differences between the American and English Oxonians. The humorist Sir Max Beerbohm, who parodied the Cult of Oxford in his 1911 novel *Zuleika Dobson*, observed that American Oxonians appeared to imbibe the customs of student life more deeply than the English themselves, becoming all the more conspicuous. "The Rhodes Scholars," noted Beerbohm, "with . . . their constant delight in all that is Oxford their English brethren don't notice . . . are a noble, rather than comfortable, element in the social life of the University." Michael Fane, the Oxonian Hero of Compton Mackenzie's *Sinister Street*, asserted that it required an American to understand completely the social aspects of Oxford life. Others admired the Rhodes men's academic seriousness. Balliol College Master A. D. Lindsay credited the presence of the American Rhodes Scholars at Balliol as a significant factor in diminishing aristocratic tendencies within the English student body.[47]

Laurence Veysey described the early twentieth century as a "season of reassessment" in American higher education. University leaders now reflected on the changes of the previous half-century. The modern university, now dressed in decidedly Gothic attire, was nevertheless committed to the advancement of scholarship and knowledge. It was also subject to the criticisms of modern social institutions; the university was now called to task for being too big, too impersonal, or too specialized. On the other side of the Atlantic stood Oxford and Cambridge; they appeared to be losing nothing to age. That was, after all, part of their appeal and charm. The more ardent admirers asserted that the ancient English universities always stood for the best contributions of the Anglo-Saxon race. To them, gravitation back toward Oxbridge was a way to reassert a more gentlemanly outlook that countered the depersonalizing forces of an increasingly corporate world. If the American research university was recent, revolutionary, bureaucratic, and impersonal, the English college was ancient, intimate, and, in the best Whig tradition, the product of an inevitable march forward. If the product of the teutonized American university of the present was an expert and a specialist, the product of the anglicized university of the near future would once more be a gentleman and scholar. Impressing Aydelotte's Oxford stamp onto the American university appeared to offer a practicable solution for supporters of the "whole man" theory who sought to find a new accommodation for undergraduate education within the university structure.[48]

3

Early Attempts

Between 1894 and 1910 unsuccessful efforts were made to establish Oxford-like systems of residential colleges at Harvard University, the University of Chicago, and Princeton University. A spirited discussion of the topic took place at Harvard, where dissidents objected to the institution's apparent lack of concern for the personal development of undergraduates. Although these critics were unable to stir Harvard's administration to action, they did elicit an exchange of opinions that illuminated the parameters of the local academic culture. The presidents of Princeton and Chicago studied the residential college idea and formulated tentative plans for its implementation, but the plans were not translated into action. Enthusiasm for residential colleges faded quickly at Chicago after President William Rainey Harper died in 1905. Two years later, Woodrow Wilson, the president of Princeton, faced resistance from alumni, faculty, and trustees over his quadrangle plan for the university.

The undergraduate student bodies at all three institutions had grown in the late nineteenth century. By the first decade of the twentieth century, the enrollments of Harvard and the University of Chicago surpassed five thousand, making them among the largest universities in the country. And at twelve hundred students, Princeton's enrollment was large by the standards of the day.[1] Since the 1860s, all three institutions had embraced research as an academic goal. Even Princeton, which maintained long-standing ties of sympathy for England, showed evidence of Teutonic influence.

In these three instances, the proponents of residential colleges had only passing acquaintance with the English pattern of higher education, and none attempted to analyze how the college system worked at either Oxford or Cambridge. At Harvard and the University of Chicago, John Corbin's *American at Oxford* (1902) was used as an authoritative source. At Princeton, Wilson used the impressions gathered on his 1896 visit to Oxford in formulating his quadrangle plan. In general, the enthusiasm for reform was never matched by detailed knowledge about the workings of the Oxbridge system.

HARVARD

Throughout the Progressive Era, Harvard University was one of the largest American institutions of higher learning and the most strongly committed to research. Enrollment in Harvard College, the university's undergraduate liberal arts school, was above 2,000 throughout the 1880s. It had the nation's largest teaching staff (573), offered more courses in a wider variety of fields than any other university, and possessed the largest library in the United States (850,000 volumes).[2] Although the faculty and administration backed the modernization that occurred during the Eliot presidency, some members of those groups felt that the positive qualities of oldtime Harvard had been lost. They particularly decried the lack of personal contact between students and faculty.

Few Harvard constituents disagreed with these critics directly. Many rationalized the lack of supervision of undergraduate life by declaring that Harvard's social "system" stressed the importance of the individual student: he determined what was in his best interest and pursued his goals according to a personal plan. William Roscoe Thayer—dean of Harvard Law School, editor of the *Harvard Graduate's Magazine,* and an avid supporter of Eliot's reforms—argued that the critics overstated the educational value of group interaction. "Those who sneer at individualism," he noted, "may be challenged to point to any great work that has not been guided by remarkable individuals. Successful team play, collective effort, and institutional progress, all presuppose that each member of the team, each unit, be the best of his kind: shall be, in other words, an expert, a specialist." Thayer compared the suggestion that a university should ignore individuals and devote itself to producing teams to a foundry that "advertised that it made a specialty of forging strong chains from weak links."[3]

But even among people who were largely satisfied with Harvard's progress, many agreed that the university lacked a vital student life. Edwin Slosson, for one, noted that students received little attention from faculty, even from those who were ostensibly their academic advisers. "In Harvard," he wrote, "the adviser is supposed to make the acquaintance of the freshmen in his charge, but this is generally a perfunctory relation, sometimes no more personal than the interpretation of the curriculum of railroad trains to the passengers in a union station."[4]

There was also concern about disunity within the student body. Harvard's student population was becoming increasingly diverse. Unlike Princeton or Yale, which drew a majority of their students from private schools, most Harvard students were graduates of public high schools. As the student body grew larger and more heterogeneous, the freshman, sophomore, junior, and senior classes became less viable as social units. Not all Harvard undergraduates chose to participate in social activities. Among those who did, the pinnacles of social attainment were the "final clubs," which served Harvard's most elite students. These were chapters of national fraternities that had broken away from their parent organizations so that members could avoid mixing with fraternity brothers from other colleges and universities. After 1865 the clubs were front organizations for social screening, and aspiring members underwent a social apprenticeship that was, as David Riesman observed, "in some ways as demanding and as disciplined as the curriculum."[5]

After Harvard in 1884 relaxed its policy of requiring that students live in campus dormitories, the social differences between students took on a spatial dimension as well. Most students abandoned the dormitories of Harvard Yard for off-campus accommodations. Many of the wealthier students took up residence in new—and expensive—private dormitories, which came to be labeled as Harvard's Gold Coast. Other students sought whatever housing they could afford: in boardinghouses, rooms in private homes, or, if they were from the Boston area, with their parents. This situation led James Anderson Hawes to conclude that Harvard lacked a real social system. What did exist, he said, was so heavily intermingled with the society of Boston's tony Back Bay that it might as well not be considered part of Harvard at all. John Corbin shared some of that sentiment but was less final in his characterization of Harvard social life. He was convinced that there indeed were positive aspects of Harvard individualism, but he thought that Harvard's social life was disorganized. He blamed the disorganization on the the faculty and alumni and their failure to regard democratic efficiency as vitally important to undergraduate life. Such critics as Lawrence Lowell saw the construction of dormitories and the reinstatement the residency requirement as ways to re-create the social cohesiveness that he assumed had existed at Harvard. Lowell believed that Harvard undergraduates would never develop a true sense of community as long as private dormitories existed.[6]

One of the earliest artifacts of this discussion was Frank

Bolles's article "An Administrative Problem," which was published by the *Harvard Graduate's Magazine* in 1894. Bolles, secretary of the Harvard Board of Overseers, was an early critic of the unitary administrative structure that Harvard developed to cope with the growing number of undergraduates. Although he did not target the English college as a model, his argument was a solid foundation for those who would follow.

Bolles maintained that if the college was too large for its dean and administrative board to manage, it should be divided into units small enough for one dean and board to know and govern effectively. He argued further that the dean and perhaps other faculty would then take up residence alongside the students. "In my judgment," noted Bolles,"nothing would add more to the quiet and respectability of dormitory life than the introduction of a Dean's family into one of the buildings under that Dean's authority. . . . If by the formation of several colleges where there is now one, it became possible not only to govern students more successfully, but to encourage their natural grouping in dormitories and around congenial dining-tables, welcome gain would be made for the present and a grave danger removed from the path of the future.[7]

Bolles' article precipitated little immediate discussion on administrative reform, but the publication of *An American at Oxford* in 1903 was followed by a revival of interest in splitting up Harvard College into residential and administrative subunits. This time the connection to Oxford was explicit. In 1904, alumnus John Fogg Twombly offered a prize to Harvard juniors and seniors for the best three essays on the "possibility and necessity of establishing a modified English college system at our large universities, with particular reference to Harvard." The winning essay, by Henry Putnam Pratt, was published the following year in the *Harvard Graduate's Magazine,* along with Twombly's own thoughts on the issue. Both writers proposed similar remedies. Twombly acknowledged that Harvard's current financial situation precluded the establishment of new residential colleges; he instead proposed organizing the existing dormitories in Harvard Yard into six "halls," each housing about one hundred twenty men. Assigning additional nonresident students to each hall would bring the number of total affiliates to about two hundred. Six or so tutors or proctors, drawn from among faculty members, would also reside in the hall. A professor would head each hall, governing it in conjunction with its elected student leaders. Members would be assigned to different eating areas within Memorial Hall (Harvard's campus dining facility) and given lockers adjacent to one another in the gymnasium. College members were also to be barred from joining any outside social clubs for the first two years of college. Twombly also suggested that the halls assume some academic functions. Sections of larger courses could be reserved for students of each hall, so that they might share a common academic experience as well as a social one. In time, halls might develop reputations for academic subjects and thereby attract students with common academic interests. The halls might then recruit tutors from those academic areas as well.[8]

Although his overall plan was similar to Twombly's, Pratt saw sport and debating, rather than academic areas, as the rallying points for identity. Pratt's essay mirrored Corbin's suggestion that the hall teams could become the breeding ground for varsity athletics. Pratt's interpretation of the hall system was reminiscent of both *An American at Oxford* and George Birkbeck Hill's idea of the college as a home. "The average undergraduate," according to Pratt, "would take his meals at one of his 'Hall' club tables in Memorial. He would listen to perhaps ten lectures a week by University professors and attend 'Hall' conferences or section meetings six or eight hours more each week. He would, it is to be hoped, divide the latter part of his afternoon between exercise on one of his 'Hall' teams and tea in his 'Hall' living room, at which as many as possible of the faculty and students of the 'Hall' would drop by."[9]

Charles Francis Adams, a faculty member, also proposed that Harvard College reorganize. In an address to Phi Beta Kappa at Columbia University in June 1906, Adams proposed replacing Harvard College with a network of residential colleges, each with a master who would know and advise his students. Praising the physical layout of the Oxbridge residential college, Adams further proposed that each Harvard college should consist of a "large household under several roofs with common grounds." He suggested establishing a variety of colleges of different clientele and academic orientation, each of which would set and charge its own fees. Harvard would then grant the final degree on the basis of examination.[10]

The following year, chemistry Professor Joseph Beale proposed the creation of a network of local colleges around the Boston area to serve as feeders to Harvard. Each college would have its own curriculum, dormitories, small library, and academic facilities. Beale thought that each college should develop its own individual character, thus offering students a choice of academic and social environments. After three years at a college, students would take a common examination; if they passed, they would be allowed to take an additional year of specialized study.[11]

In the course of this discussion, Lawrence Lowell, then a professor of political science, emerged as the most important backer of the residential college idea. Lowell asserted that the English college model was superior to the American fraternity in providing students with opportunities for social growth. Although fraternities did foster some social development among their members, Lowell acknowledged, they could not provide the same kind of fellowship as the English college because membership was restricted to a small segment of the undergraduate population and tended to exacerbate geographical differences among the students. Lowell advocated the creation of a residential system in which undergraduates could meet on common ground and on a human scale. His solution was to reorganize Harvard into several residential colleges, each a microcosm of the student body as a whole. Lowell also proposed that all students have a common experience in freshman residence halls so that they could mix with one another before choosing a college, thus undoing the tendency for boys who prepped together to remain in their cliques.[12]

Although the proponents of residential colleges failed to bring about any administrative action on behalf of their ideas, they did elicit strong responses from defenders of Harvard individualism. Rebutting one of John Corbin's *Saturday Evening Post* articles criticizing Harvard's social life, historian Albert Bushnell Hart asserted that Harvard students did not need the university to legislate a social system for them. He further denigrated the college idea because he felt that it would damage the university's cohesiveness. "The English system," noted Hart, "not only subdivides the students, but the teachers; not only makes colleges, but dissolves the university."[13]

William R. Thayer also criticized the proponents of residential colleges, whom he felt exaggerated the educational effects of the colleges. "One panacea prescribed by some critics," he argued, "is Oxfordization—the adoption of the Oxford system of residential halls or colleges, each with its kitchen and commons and dons." Thayer acknowledged that the residential college system worked well in England, but he observed that the lack of an alternative model resulted in unfounded attributions about the effects of living in college. "To listen to its advocates," he argued, "one would suppose that Macaulay and

Gladstone . . . could never have amounted to anything had they not eaten dinner in hall."[14]

Although no action was seriously contemplated by the Eliot administration regarding the college ideas, Eliot himself addressed the question in his report for 1906–7. He found little merit to the suggestions, noting the considerable expense of a college plan and the problems presented by the separate ownership and control of university property by the colleges. Eliot concluded that if the point of these ideas was to imitate the "relations, pecuniary and social, of an English undergraduate to his tutor," then they presented "considerable difficulty."[15] Building dormitories was expensive enough in and of itself; to erect facilities that would meet the requirements of a residential college system meant a prohibitively large expenditure. In the early twentieth century, this was beyond Harvard's financial resources, and no private donor appeared ready underwrite such a venture.

The University of Chicago

Unlike Harvard, which was three centuries old at the turn of the century, the University of Chicago was one of the youngest institutions of higher learning in America. The growth of the "University on the Midway" had been rapid. In 1907, just fifteen years after its founding, the university enrolled 4,550 students, 2,439 of whom were undergraduates.[16] President Harper was dedicated to creating the most modern institution that Rockefeller money could buy. His first priorities had been to obtain the best faculty available and to establish his university as an outstanding center for scholarly research. He also wanted to establish a strong residential undergraduate program, a commitment reflected in the original physical specifications of the university. The plans, drawn by Henry Ives Cobb, devoted more than half of the floor space of the campus to dormitories.[17]

The University of Chicago had something of a split personality: it was a germanized research university encased in one of the most extensive reproductions of Oxford-style college buildings ever attempted. Its architecture was among the most thoroughly Gothic of any American university's, perhaps counting only Princeton's as a rival. The ambitious building program included several structures that were almost copies of English medieval buildings. Dean George Vincent resolved the apparent contradiction between German and English influences by explaining that the "university takes pride in her laboratories, but she also covets for her students something of the charmed life of the cloisters." Other observers asserted that Harper and his associates were eager to compensate for their institution's youth by using whatever means were at their disposal. Edwin Slosson, himself a Chicago Ph.D., thought his alma mater reeked of academic pretension: "The University of Chicago," he contended, "does not look its age. It looks much older." To Slosson, the result of this "artificial aging process" was a "pseudo-antique" campus, one that gave "visible emphasis to the already exaggerated distinction between men who have certain degrees and men who have them not."[18]

Behind the Gothic edifices, however, was a genuine spirit of undergraduate curricular innovation. It included a new organizational scheme that attempted to create a logical transition between the generalism of an academic secondary education and the specialized instruction associated with graduate work. The four-class system was replaced by "junior" and "senior" colleges, each with a distinct pedagogical focus. Instruction in the junior college, which covered the first and second year of undergraduate work, was geared toward the completion of the general educational program that was presumed to have begun in secondary school. The specialized academic work in the senior college would be would be connected to the graduate curriculum.[19]

Efforts were also made to establish an active social environment for undergraduates. A residential system was organized in 1893, when the dormitories were subdivided into "houses." A house in this context was understood to mean a group of members of the university who were entitled to occupancy in a particular unit of residence. Each house was to be governed by a head (chosen by the university president), a counselor (chosen from the faculty by the members of the house), and an elected house committee. Each house was expected to develop an identity, traditions, and good-natured rivalries with other houses. Six houses were established in 1893, and two were added later. In its original form, the house plan bore a strong resemblance to the fraternity system; in fact, by 1902 twelve fraternity chapters had been incorporated as university houses. By 1900 three houses had been organized for day students, although they functioned as clubs rather than as residential units.[20]

The architects of the house plan showed a clear predilection for the Oxford image. In the *Decennial Report of the University of Chicago* (1903), Director of Residence James Thompson maintained that the goal of the house system was to facilitate the acquisition of a "four-square" education. In his report Thompson strongly reflected Arnold's—and Corbin's—ideals of balance. The optimal education, he wrote, should incorporate liberal arts, science, gymnastics, and the "manners that make the man." He believed that contemporary higher education was deficient on two accounts. First, it failed to appreciate the positive value that "physical culture" (that is, athletic competition) added to the intellectual efforts of academic course work. Second, contemporary colleges failed to adequately develop the "social instinct in the student during the formative period of life, when character is most adaptable and the lessons of experience are most easily learned."[21]

Thompson further emphasized the value of the "broad sympathetic social life" of the residential hall. He noted that a residential structure could provide a strong social foundation for students, out which a sense of common intellectual purpose could then arise. He saw meals as an important component in this process. "Table talk," he argued, "is doubtless one of the most ancient forms of literature, and now as always one of the most universal. Man relaxes as he eats, and becomes social."[22]

Thompson's thoughts also had much in common with Corbin's notion of the residence hall providing a homelike atmosphere, and, like Corbin, he looked to the Oxford colleges as an organizational exemplar. "The most ideal institution of learning, so far as the *home* is concerned, is Oxford, where the colleges are only houses developed." Thompson echoed Corbin's prescription for success: first, the hall ought to serve only a limited membership; second, it should possess a common dining room, meeting and recreational space; third, the body of the house should control the selection of new members; and fourth, house members should feel a sense of ownership over property. Thompson proposed that the head of the house, who would have coequal status with the academic deans, would be a member of the faculty, appointed by the university president.[23] The selection of new members was to be determined by the existing membership.

Expanding the house system into an Oxford-like network of residential colleges was suggested to Harper by Vincent, who was dean of the junior college. In 1901, Vincent acquainted Harper with *An American at Oxford,* and he proposed that an Oxbridge-inspired system of residential colleges might be a worthwhile addition to the academic program. In keeping with Corbin's concern for the continuity of communities, Vincent further proposed the establishment of a fellowship system that would subsidize students who remained in the halls during their graduate study. Their presence would help strengthen student identity with the house by providing continuity.[24]

Unlike his counterparts at Harvard, President Harper was only too happy to investigate the feasibility of a system of residential colleges. In September 1902 he sent the ailing Dean Ernest DeWitt Burton to Europe as a vacation from his teaching duties. While in England, Burton visited Oxford and was given an insider's look at the university. Although his trip was not intended as a full-scale investigation of the English university system, Burton communicated to Harper that little at Oxford could be reproduced.[25]

Nevertheless, Harper became interested in combining the academic strengths of the junior college with the social promise of the house system. Part of the impetus came from the realization that the small-college atmosphere that had characterized the undergraduate program during its first decade evaporated as the university grew. The same impersonality that Frank Bolles had seen at Harvard now existed at Chicago. By the middle of the decade, the growth of university enrollment had made such a plan even more desirable. In 1905, Harper proposed refashioning the junior college into eight quadrangles, each housing about 175 students. Each quadrangle would consist of four residential halls, plus classrooms, studios, and laboratories. In contrast with Lowell's idea of residential colleges containing a cross section of undergraduates, the Chicago quadrangles were to separate students by course of study and sex. Four quadrangles were to be for men, and four were for women. Among the men's and women's groupings would be one quadrangle each for students studying arts, literature, philosophy, and science. The existing residential facilities were included in the plan, but additional halls would also be required.[26]

Harper's plan did not provoke the kind of retorts received by proponents of residential colleges at Harvard. Not surprisingly, Edwin Slosson criticized the idea of segregating students by course of study. He maintained that students would be unable to mix freely with people of their own choosing, and he pointed out that the fraternities at the university had achieved some success in social education by attracting a more diversified group.[27]

These plans were not carried out. Harper died in October 1905, leaving the residential college idea without a powerful advocate. But even if Harper had lived, the plan might still have foundered. The University of Chicago faced the same sorts of financial constraints as Harvard, despite Harper's freewheeling expenditures. Harry Pratt Judson, Harper's successor, had to contend with competing institutional priorities, and there was no money to build the additional quadrangles.

PRINCETON

In 1907, Woodrow Wilson threw down a gauntlet to the upholders of tradition at Princeton. "For all its subtle charm and beguiling air of academic distinction," he wrote in his "Report on the Social Co-ordination of the University," "Princeton, so far as her undergraduates are concerned, had come to be merely a delightful place of residence."[28] But Wilson was attracted to the residential college pattern for different reasons than were Harper or the Harvard proponents. Unlike at Harvard or Chicago, undergraduate social life thrived at Princeton. Wilson sought to make the students' world more attuned to academic values.

Princeton enrolled about one-third as many students as Harvard or the University of Chicago, and many of its alumni and faculty held strongly to its old-time collegiate heritage.[29] Tradition endured even though Princeton (called the College of New Jersey until 1896) underwent significant change as it became a modern university. During the long presidency of James McCosh (1868–1898), scholarships and fellowships were established, an impressive library was created, a graduate program was initiated, and faculty were encouraged to pursue research.[30] Although he followed a course of expansion resembling those at Harvard and Chicago, McCosh resisted the idea of Princeton becoming a germanized university. He insisted on trying to create what he called an "Oxford-like intellectual atmosphere." The shift in mission was accompanied by a shift in governance as control of the university moved from the Presbyterian Church to the university's alumni, who became increasingly organized and an important source of financial support. By the beginning of the twentieth century, alumni clubs and trustees constituted a powerful interest group in Princeton's internal politics, and a critical source of support — or opposition — to presidential plans.[31]

The tenuousness of adopting the modern research university ideal within an Oxford-like intellectual atmosphere carried over after McCosh retired in 1898. Like many educators of the time, McCosh's successor, Francis Landey Patton (1898–1902), believed that only a small minority of students was seriously interested in academics. His unwillingness to initiate reform despite a faculty call for higher academic standards led to his resignation. Patton's replacement was Woodrow Wilson, whose educational philosophy had much in common with Patton's and McCosh's. He earnestly believed, however, that the proportion of the studious could be increased if the environment was molded to suit such a purpose.[32]

Tension between the social life of students and the academic expectations of faculty was something of a Princeton tradition. In the early nineteenth century, student life had centered around the Whig and Cliosophic literary societies. In the 1840s, after enrollments expanded, ten Greek-letter fraternities established chapters clandestinely. These were small organizations, rarely exceeding ten members, but they were feared by the faculty because, unlike the literary societies, they existed beyond the pale of parietal supervision. In 1855, in response to the growth of fraternities, the faculty and trustees mandated that all matriculating students promise not to join any secret organization. The fraternities were finally eradicated in 1875. Since the 1860s undergraduate social life had been dominated by Princeton's twelve eating clubs, which owned and operated their own houses and provided meals and social life for their members.[33]

The dominance of the eating clubs—nonsecret but still exclusive—increased along with the growing popularity of college athletics, primarily football. The importance of social life at Princeton was further abetted by a shift in the composition of the student body: in the late 1800s the number of students preparing for the ministry dropped while the number of students from wealthy backgrounds rose. In the 1890s the clubs constructed elaborate homes that included dining rooms, billiard rooms, sleeping quarters for alumni, and libraries.[34] To Edwin Slosson, the opulence of the eating club rendered the objection to Greek-letter societies nonsensical. He observed that the clubs were just as "luxurious, engrossing and exclusive as the fraternities." John Corbin praised them as the university's most valuable social asset.[35]

The typical Princetonian of the early twentieth century was, in Slosson's assessment, a little like Peter Pan, "not quite grown up, and not quite wanting to be. . . . The Princetonian does not seem to care whether school keeps or not; but this is not a cynical affectation of indifference, it is the natural indifference of irresponsible and careless boyishness." Horseplay was apparently more common at Princeton than at other universities. The effort to gain eating club membership could be as strenuous as penetrating Harvard's socially elite student organizations. Rather than take their chances as individuals, underclassmen organized themselves into associations called hat lines and then applied for membership to the eating clubs as groups. Princeton-bound seniors at preparatory schools that regularly sent students to the university were the leaders of some of hat lines.[36]

Wilson saw the emulation of Oxford as a way to move the social world of Princeton toward a more academic orientation. He drew some of his inspiration from his lifelong fascination with England. "No studies delighted him," biographer Ray Stannard Baker wrote, "as keenly as those of English historical heroes." Some of his utterances on education might just as easily have come from Jowett, Newman, or Arnold. Like Jowett, Wilson apparently envisioned the college as the producer of a class of public servants in the spirit of Balliol College and Oxford. Like Arnold, he believed in the propagation, through acculturation, of an active class of "gentlemen" to help purify the national life. Like Newman, he believed that the objects of a university were intellectual and that all else was incidental or corollary. Further, he felt, like Newman, that residence under college auspices would "tame and refine individual spirits."[37] Like Lowell and Newman, Wilson believed strongly in self-education. To him, teaching was a matter of advice and guidance provided by those more mature and experienced to those less so. It was therefore a matter of intellectual companionship and joint participation in the pursuit of learning. J. Duncan Spaeth, who served on the Princeton faculty under Wilson, remembered in 1946 that "whenever I read Matthew Arnold's testimony to the influence of Newman at Oxford, I recollect the voice of Woodrow Wilson."[38]

Wilson said that his ideas for reforming Princeton along English lines dated back to 1897. His 1896 visit to England left him with generally positive impressions of the country, it nevertheless reinforced his American identity. He was utterly taken with Oxford, however. He wrote to his wife, Ellen, that "Oxford is enough to take one's heart by storm. . . . I am afraid that if there were a place for me here, America would only see me again to sell the house and to fetch you and the children."[39]

There were three phases to Wilson's attempted reform of Princeton. The first was a comprehensive reorganization of the curriculum. The second was the establishment of a modified tutorial plan, called the preceptorial system. In the third phase, Princeton's organizational pattern was to be remodeled into a system of residential colleges. The first two components of reform were overwhelmingly successful, bolstering Wilson's belief that he could take on more large-scale reforms with the unquestioned backing of the university's trustees. Once his reform agenda left the academic realm, however, a powerful alliance of faculty and alumni members of the Board of Trustees emerged to oppose Wilson's plans.

The academic reorganization was accompanied by a restructuring of the undergraduate course of study. Under McCosh, Princeton had in 1868 adopted a limited elective system for upperclassmen. Wilson desired to increase the number of electable courses so that student programs could culminate in some kind of advanced study, but he followed solidly in McCosh's footsteps in opposing Harvard-style free election. In 1903 all professors were grouped in twelve departments that in turn were organized into four divisions: philosophy, art and archaeology, language and literature, mathematics and science. These new divisions undergirded the new undergraduate course of study, which was adopted in 1904. The freshman year remained prescribed, but during the sophomore year students were granted some choice between fundamental courses. At the beginning of the junior year students were required to complete a distributed number of upper-level courses and to choose a primary course of study. During the senior year all courses were in the student's chosen area of study.[40]

The curricular reform was a precursor to the preceptorial plan, a modified form of the Oxford tutorial that aimed to "import to the great university the methods and personal contact of the small college and so gain the advantages of both."[41] Wilson believed there could be no true intellectual life at Princeton until students reflected on the curriculum outside of the classroom. He also believed that Princeton students would gladly follow an intellectual path that offered respite from the demands of the prevailing social environment. The system was based on a new type of faculty member—the preceptor—whose primary responsibility was to engage students in an individualized academic relationship, much like the one that Wilson envisioned between Oxford tutors and undergraduates. The relationship between preceptor and student would bridge the gap between the curriculum and students' lives. According to the plan, junior- and senior-level students and preceptors were assigned to a weekly group tutorial that focused on readings collateral with the student's lectures. The preceptors were to be selected "primarily on their standing as gentlemen, as men who are companionable, clubable, whose personal qualities of association give them influence over the minds of younger men," Wilson wrote.[42]

Wilson believed that the preceptorial plan was a genuine improvement on the English system. He had criticized the Oxbridge practice of appointing tutors for life because he felt that it allowed tutors to shirk their responsibilities for more congenial tasks. But the preceptor's duties, as Wilson conceived them, were not identical to those of the tutors, who job was to help develop the students' capacities to undertake specialized scholarship. Wilson was looking for men whose personalities and life experiences would enable them to influence students beyond the intellectual sphere. Importantly, Wilson was not looking for scholars, or scholars-to-be, to perform this role. He first attempted to offer the positions to schoolmasters, but he was unable to persuade any of the men he approached to accept preceptorial posts. Wilson was persuaded by Dean Henry Fine to look for academics instead.[43]

The lack of adequate funding was an additional stumbling block. Wilson was nevertheless able to capitalize on the trustees' confidence in him that came in the wake of the successful curricular reorganization. An emergency fund of $100,000 a year for three years was established to initiate the program. In 1905, the trustees officially established the title "preceptor." Forty-five men became preceptors at the rank of assistant professor: twelve were already on campus, and Wilson recruited the remainder from other institutions. Thirty-seven of the first forty-nine preceptors appointed had doctoral degrees.[44]

The preceptorial system and the curricular reorganization were almost immediately hailed as great successes, buoying Wilson's confidence in his ability to pursue the rest of his reform agenda. The third component of Wilson's reform, the quadrangle plan, took aim at the social side of Princeton organization and brought Wilson into intense conflict with Princeton alumni, faculty and students. Wilson sought to create a "college comradeship based on letters." He called the club system a major obstacle to overcoming the dichotomy between Princeton's social and academic life, saying that the clubs "are now in danger of embarrassing and even profoundly demoralizing the life of the University." Beyond the attention that students lavished on the club system, Wilson was concerned that the clubs divided all four classes into segments, sharply separating members from nonmembers and upperclassmen from underclassmen. About one-third of the sophomore class was not selected for club membership, and Wilson described their lot as "deplorable."[45]

In his "Report on the Social Co-ordination of the University" delivered to the trustees in October 1907, Wilson proposed reorganizing the undergraduate student body into four residential quadrangles, each with unmarried faculty in residence as masters and preceptors. The social life of each quadrangle would center on a common dining hall and common room. As in the English college, the goal of the quadrangle system was to mix younger and older students. Students would be assigned to a quadrangle by the university upon matriculation. In the process of reorganizing the campus residence system, the eating clubs would either be abolished or absorbed into the quadrangle system. Wilson also commissioned blueprints to show how the club buildings could expand into quadrangles. The estimated cost for the project was $2 million.[46]

A significant difference between Wilson's scheme and Chicago's plan was that the Princeton quadrangles lacked ties to the curricular scheme of the college. The role of the resident faculty, like that of the preceptors, reflected Wilson's belief that spontaneous contact between older and younger men could play a powerful educative role. According to Wilson, implementation of the quadrangle plan would bring faculty into "close, habitual, natural association with the undergraduates and so intimately tie the intellectual and social life of the place into one another."[47]

Although initial reactions to the quadrangle plan suggested to Wilson that faculty and alumni support was forthcoming, opposition began to mount within these groups. Several trustees balked at the price tag even though they did not support the clubs. Many alumni, including some faculty members and the editors of the *Princeton Alumni Weekly,* opposed the dismantling of the club system.

Wilson's chief political rival, Graduate Dean Andrew West, and West's powerful ally on the Board of Trustees, former U.S. President Grover Cleveland, did not want to see West's pet project, a graduate residential college, shelved in favor of the undergraduate quadrangles. West's opposition was clearly a matter of differing institutional priorities. Indeed, as Laurence Veysey observed, Wilson and West held similar views on many aspects of higher education, and the men shared a strong attachment to England and English culture. West had enthusiastically supported the adoption of Gothic as Princeton's architectural style in the 1890s and had backed the preceptorial plan.[48]

Even after resistance began to mount in the summer of 1907, Wilson refused to heed the advice of associates who suggested that he compromise to achieve some of his objectives. In October 1907, when the trustees voted to ask Wilson to withdraw his plan, he sought other means to gain support. Wilson continued, unsuccessfully, to argue his case to Princeton alumni. In 1909 he nearly secured $3.5 million from the Carnegie Foundation for the plan, but the proposal was personally quashed by Andrew Carnegie.[49]

The postmortem on the quadrangle plan yielded varied opinions. Lawrence Lowell believed that Wilson's inability to compromise led to the demise of a plan that a wiser politician might have salvaged.[50] However, Lowell did not agree with all of Wilson's ideas: he thought that, even if the plan were adopted, the quadrangles' inability to choose their own members, in the fashion of Oxbridge colleges, would have remained a central problem. James Anderson Hawes thought that Wilson's plan was too simplistic and failed to take into account the practical details of Princeton's organization, especially the disposition of the clubs' properties, which did not belong to Princeton. John Corbin, an Anglophile par excellence, in turn criticized the plan because he felt that the clubs, with their emphasis on social life and tradition, already provided Princeton with a strong link to the residential college pattern of Oxford. The clubs, wrote Corbin, "have their origin deep in the instincts of Princeton life, and have a long and most honorable association with the Princeton spirit at its best. . . . To put the axe to the root of the system is to blight much that is most precious in the moral life of the institution." Corbin further asserted that Wilson under-valued the effect of residence halls. He believed that the experience a student gained by living in residence halls for the first two years would minimize the negative influences of the clubs without destroying any positive aspects.[51]

The preceptorial plan lasted longer than Wilson's presidency but was substantially modified to conform to subsequent curricular reform. In 1908, Abraham Flexner expressed doubt that the system offered a sound or adequate substructure. Over time, his concerns proved correct. The preceptors were burdened with reading for too many courses, and they lacked time for their own scholarly endeavors. The system also did not engender the kind of independent study originally intended. By 1925 the titles were no longer in use, and academic department advisers took over the tutorials.[52]

The watershed of West's political victory was the construction of the graduate college, which was designed in the Gothic style by Ralph Adams Cram. West fought for and won an Oxbridge-style residential college for fifty graduate students rather than for twelve hundred undergraduates. The defeat of the quadrangle plan and the subsequent losing battle over the location of the graduate college were the final acts in Wilson's presidency. In 1910, upon receiving the Democratic Party nomination for the governorship of New Jersey, he resigned to pursue a political career.

Even though these overtures did not result in the adoption of the residential college idea, the proposals remained influential in some quarters. The primary reason that the residential college idea sputtered in the 1900s was because it demanded too serious a reconsideration of institutional priorities. Whether or not this was the intention of residential college proponents, their plans, if implemented, would require the redirection of effort away from academic reform and expansion of research-oriented activities toward the construction of new residential buildings, the implementation of new academic organizations, and, in the case of Princeton, the creation of a new variety of teacher. Although the rhetoric of William Rainey Harper might incorporate an increased commitment to research and the development of undergraduate culture, the resources to carry out all of those tasks were not readily forthcoming, at Chicago or elsewhere. Resistance to residential colleges on financial grounds was, in fact, a common denominator of all three attempts.

Another common denominator to the residential college proposals was the absence of systematic study of how Oxford and Cambridge actually operated. In all three cases Oxford was viewed through the lenses of Arnold and Newman, whether interpreted by Corbin or Wilson. Occasional visits to Oxford did not clarify anyone's vision. At Chicago, Ernest Burton's trip to England was primarily for rest, not to gather information on Oxford. He did not even provide Harper with a detailed report of his visit. At Princeton, Wilson formulated his plans on decade-old recollections of a visit to Oxford. That these proponents of the residential college idea appeared to lack an understanding of the details of Oxford governance was not lost on Edwin Slosson, who noted quizzically in 1910 that the "particular thing we are most anxious to get from Oxford and Cambridge, their residential colleges, is what reformers in these universities are most anxious to break up."[53]

There were, however, some distinctly American wrinkles in the residential college idea. American proponents had to devise ways to make the residential college square with the organization of academic departments. Two solutions were proposed. The first, proposed by some advocates at Harvard and adopted by Harper at Chicago, was to create residential colleges with curricular foci. This may have reflected contemporary American notions of organizational efficiency rather than the English pattern of each college maintaining its own faculty. The second solution, advocated by Wilson, was to dispense with college-based instruction altogether and to rely on the educative power of informal contact between student and teacher.

At least one critic saw the whole movement as a wild goose chase that sidestepped the problems of contemporary undergraduate education. Abraham Flexner criticized plans to Oxfordize the university because they did not help clarify the purpose of an undergraduate education. "So far," he noted, "propositions that endeavor to face the problem have looked at it from the administrative or social side. Now the administrative problem may perhaps be solved by sub-dividing the overgrown college into several bodies. . . . The social problem may be solved by housing the students in residential colleges of the Oxford type. But these devices do not touch the pedagogical problem."[54]

The burst of enthusiasm in bringing Oxbridge to America might well have ended in 1907. Neither Princeton nor the University of Chicago ever again ventured down that path. But at Harvard, where proponents were not taken as seriously, the idea stayed in circulation, thanks in part to the persistence of Lawrence Lowell and like-minded men. Residential colleges were seen by many as too expensive, out of line with the immediate needs of the institutions in question, or irrelevant to the real problems of higher education. At the same time, however, Lowell, who became president of Harvard in 1909, maintained that the American university needed more social life among its students. Something was still needed to provide undergraduates with a homelike atmosphere that would span the widening rift between student and scholar. However, competing demands for institutional resources directed money away from solutions based on interpretations of Oxbridge.

4

The Harkness Bequests

HARVARD HOUSES AND YALE COLLEGES

At its inception in 1929, Harvard University's house plan was described as a "Princeton plan done at Harvard with Yale money."[1] The surprise decision of Yale alumnus and oil millionaire Edward Harkness to fund a system of residential houses made possible Lawrence Lowell's long-held dream of establishing a system of Oxbridge-like colleges at Harvard. Harvard's houses—and the Harkness-funded residential colleges at Yale that followed two years later—were intended to foster coherent social life in what had become primarily nonresidential universities. The facilitation of contact between undergraduate students and between students and faculty (a reflection of the ideas of Woodrow Wilson) was of utmost importance. Although such proponents as Yale President James Rowland Angell envisioned a more explicit connection between the residential college and the formal curriculum, residential college plans relied heavily on the assumption that housing faculty and students under one roof would help generate an intellectually stimulating atmosphere.

Although these efforts were an attempt to address larger developments that were deemed hostile to the "spirit" of Harvard and Yale of earlier decades, they were also consistent with a new emphasis on undergraduate education at many research-oriented universities in the 1920s. Up until World War I the idea of eliminating or reducing the undergraduate curriculum at institutions like Harvard and Yale still enjoyed some degree of consideration. After that time, however, concern for the state of undergraduate experience—both curricular and extra-curricular—occupied center stage.[2]

This increasing emphasis on undergraduate education was complemented by a rise in enrollments at Harvard and Yale Colleges. Between 1910 and 1923, Yale's entering class grew from 302 students to 886. In roughly the same period (1909-1922), the annual number of students admitted to Harvard College rose from 551 to 698. The increased demand for places in the entering classes prompted both institutions to cap freshman enrollments and to reformulate their admissions policies. Before 1916, Harvard and Yale administered their own entrance examinations, admitting most of the applicants who met the published admissions requirements. In that year both institutions replaced their tests with sophisticated competitive admissions procedures.[3]

The new procedures did not aim to restrict enrollment to the most academically qualified students. Other characteristics of the student bodies—particularly ethnicity, race, and sex—concerned the schools. By 1920 the older admissions policies at Harvard had produced an influx of Jewish students, many of whom were the children of Eastern European immigrants. In the eyes of men like Lawrence Lowell, who believed that many Jews resisted assimilation into the common American Culture, these new students threatened the social composition of the student body. Although Lowell remained committed to using undergraduate residences to ensure interaction between different types of students, his definition of acceptable student types restricted the number of Jews at Harvard and excluded African-Americans. Despite some resistance from Harvard faculty and students, he was able to institute informal admissions quotas for these students that remained in place until the 1950s. During the Lowell presidency the small number of African-American students faced discrimination that was unknown under Eliot.[4] In 1914 they were barred from residence in newly constructed dormitories. Although this ban was rescinded in 1923 under public pressure, segregation within Harvard dormitories continued until after World War II.[5]

Yale's administration was likewise concerned about the increasing number of Jewish students. In May 1918, Dean Frederick S. Jones expressed his fear that Yale College might be "overrun" if action was not taken to limit the number of Jewish undergraduates. In the early 1920s, Jones and other administrators quietly enacted informal quotas on the numbers of Jews admitted to Yale College. A ceiling on the amount of scholarship money awarded to Jewish students also enabled Yale to "stabilize" its Jewish enrollment.[6]

As Harvard and Yale grew in size, and as their administrators worried about the increasingly diverse student bodies, interest in Oxbridge grew more intense. Fears about the impact of immigration from non-northern European countries—characterized by such contemporary events as the imposition of immigration quotas and the Sacco-Vanzetti case—fueled the notion of an Anglo-Saxon–rooted American cultural identity. British society was romantically perceived as revering the past, yielding to change slowly and carefully. Public fascination with the Oxford mystique was similarly strong, with many Americans continuing to believe that Oxford had perfected its educational apparatus only after centuries of evolution. In this vein, contemporary humorist Stephen Leacock noted that Oxford, although it had "no order, no arrangement," and "no system," was nevertheless able to give to its students "a life and mode of thought" that Americans could "emulate, but not yet equal."[7]

Within academe, the constant flow of Rhodes Scholars out of Oxford and into American institutions of higher education—and the enduring concern for the size and impersonality of research universities—fueled interest in the order and arrangement of English universities. Despite enthusiasm for English-inspired innovations, few institutions investigated the actual workings of Oxford or Cambridge. An exception to this trend was Dartmouth College, which sent chemistry professor Leon B. Richardson to England in 1923 to study several universities. Richardson devoted far more attention to Oxford than any other institution, and his conclusions clearly sought to temper any enthusiasm for Oxfordization at Dartmouth.[8]

Richardson disagreed with the ideas put forward by John Corbin a quarter-century earlier, observing that the "system of Oxford and Cambridge, which has for so long been held up to American institutions as an example of a well balanced division between things of the body and the mind, is regarded by many [British educators] as a huge over-development and over-emphasis of things essentially trivial." He asserted that many features of the British system ought only to be considered "in the light of examples to avoid." Richardson did praise some aspects of Oxbridge practice, but those he valued most highly were the least likely to be of interest to the proponents of residential colleges, particularly the ability of the English system to develop exceptional students as highly qualified academic specialists. He held little confidence that Dartmouth could profit by following the example of Oxford, and concluded that "on the whole the American College is so organized and so rooted that there seems to be little chance of imposing on it a system which, however good may be its success in its natural environment, is not indigenous to our soil."[9]

Lawrence Lowell maintained his faith in the educative power of the Oxonian ideal, however. Although he particularly lamented Harvard's lack of the kind of broad scholarship frequently associated with English universities,[10] Lowell—like John Corbin and George Birkbeck Hill—believed that Harvard's strong academic base could be combined with aspects of Oxford's pattern of instruction to produce a system superior to that in either country. Lowell also felt strongly that the fragmentation of the curriculum had decreased undergraduates' consciousness of the value of a liberal education. While students might see connections between excellence in the professional school and success in their future careers, they did not see a similar connection between the intellectual training of a liberal arts college and success in life. He asserted that this was less true in England, where liberal education was seen as appropriate preparation for professional or academic life.[11] Lowell saw a structured residential experience, organized along lines similar to those of an Oxford college, as a way to immerse students in an environment that meet their intellectual and social needs. Faced with an increasingly diverse population and student body, he reasserted the view, articulated earlier by Matthew Arnold and Woodrow Wilson, that the common life of a residential college could help to cultivate a democratic elite that was intellectually and socially fit to govern. As Laurence Veysey noted, Lowell saw democracy as "something that was realized in the presence of a homogeneous mass of gentlemen."[12]

During the two decades following his inauguration in 1909, Lowell led efforts to create a more coherent and orderly undergraduate curriculum, and to provide an academic environment conducive to the tenets of "self-education." The first of these steps occurred in 1910, when a system of concentration and distribution requirements replaced the free elective system, which had been the cornerstone of the undergraduate program during Eliot's tenure.[13] Lowell and his associates also pursued other measures aimed at adapting features of the Oxbridge pattern

The Harkness Bequests / 95

to Harvard. These efforts included the adoption of tutorial systems and general examinations, and an increased commitment to residential living.

After the concentration and distribution requirements were instituted, Lowell pressed for departmental comprehensive examinations and a system of tutorial instruction. These measures aimed to ensure that students acquired a thorough knowledge of their subject of concentration and provided an incentive for intellectual effort to Harvard College's academically lackadaisical students.[14] Following Lowell's initiatives, the Division of History, Government, and Economics in 1912 introduced tutorial work and general examinations. Beginning in the sophomore year, each student was assigned to a tutor in his field of concentration. The tutor worked with the student until his senior year, when the student took general examinations. In 1919, Harvard's faculty decided that all departments so willing could establish general examinations within their areas. Between 1919 and 1924 all but two academic departments (chemistry and engineering sciences) instituted general examinations coupled with tutorial instruction.[15] Harvard was not the only institution interested in such programs. Comprehensive examinations—with or without tutorial instruction—had been growing in popularity since the turn of the century. The number of colleges and universities using these examinations increased from 7 in 1900 to 71 in 1925. By 1935, this number had grown to 242.[16]

In spite of a clear attempt to emulate English practice, Harvard's tutorial plan bore only superficial similarity to the Oxonian interplay between student and don. Since the Harvard undergraduate program did not aim to cultivate academic specialists, this arrangement did not place the tutor in the commanding educational role he enjoyed in England. Even with concentration and distribution requirements, the academic program at Harvard College was still highly elective in nature, so that the Harvard tutor largely supplemented, rather than directed, the student's educational program.[17]

The departmental structure of the American university further hindered Harvard's ability to replicate the relationship between the Oxonian tutor and undergraduate. Tutorial arrangements, staffing, and the importance placed on the tutorial itself varied from department to department. Some used graduate students as tutors, and others employed full faculty; some emphasized the tutorial as a major component of the concentration, and others played down its importance. Despite the Oxbridge pedagogical ideal Lowell sought to create, Harvard College students often found themselves with inexperienced or uninterested tutors.[18]

Some members of the Harvard faculty did attempt to confer with their Oxford counterparts regarding the mechanics of the tutorial system. In 1924, after Harvard's English department decided to adopt tutorial instruction, two junior faculty members were sent to Oxford to observe the system in action. Because of their teaching responsibilities, the men did not arrive in England until summer, when Oxford was not in session, so they saw little of the tutorial system in operation. H. P. Perkins, a Rhodes Scholar from 1923–26 at Queen's College, described the visit, speculating that the Oxford tutors were in all likelihood astonished by the goals of Harvard's tutorial plan. According to Perkins, the ideas behind the American conception of a tutor were "sufficiently remote from the real basis . . . to make it rather difficult for an Englishman . . . to answer their questions in his own sense." This divergence in understanding made it "difficult for the Englishman to indicate his profound disagreement with the informal, ultra-personal view of education." Perkins also lampooned what he saw as inappropriate reverence toward the tutorial system: "There is much delightful talk from the tutors. . . . This tends to nourish the idea that a tutorial is ringed with tobacco smoke and incubates 'personal contact.' [The American observer] is probably familiar with Stephen Leacock's picture of intellectual osmosis in a tutorial: there is no activity . . . except puffing at a pipe, and yet somehow at the end of four years an enormous amount of something valuable has been conveyed to the student. . . . This view is promulgated so widely that one is tempted to ask why the Pullman smoker has not been accepted as the school for American youth."[19]

Lowell achieved greater success in the area of student housing. Between 1914 and 1918 his dream of new freshman halls was realized, coupled with a faculty advisory system for new undergraduate students.[20] The four residence halls provided lodging for more than five hundred freshmen. By the standards of the day, the accommodations were luxurious. Instead of the cramped rooms arrayed along corridors in the barracks fashion found at other colleges and universities, the living quarters for the freshmen consisted of suites of single rooms that shared a common sitting room with its own fireplace. Each of the freshman halls contained a dining room, common rooms, and—at the insistence of the president—large comfortable chairs. The attractiveness of these new quarters was also intended to woo some of Harvard's most socially elite students out of their digs on the Gold Coast. Corresponding with the opening of the first of these halls in 1914, Harvard instituted regulations that required most students (excluding African-Americans) to live in the halls during their freshman year. This requirement weakened the position of the Gold Coast dormitories, which managed to stay in operation for only a few more years. During World War I, Harvard bought the private residence halls and incorporated them into its residential system.[21]

Lowell also tried to restore the residential character of Harvard Yard. To address the problems that prompted the student exodus in the 1880s, all residence halls, old and new, were, for the first time in Harvard's history, supplied with bathrooms, a development that Dean LeBaron Russell Briggs called a "belated tribute to modern civilization." Between 1923 and 1925 new dormitories were added to the perimeter of Harvard Yard, creating a quadrangle of sorts out of the core of the Harvard campus. As architectural historian Paul V. Turner observed, "The wall of buildings served the practical function of screening the Yard from the noise . . . of Cambridge, but it also embodied the new desire for cloistered collegiality."[22]

The desire for collegial intimacy was also in evidence at Yale University. Although faculty and administrators did not show strong interest in Oxford-style curricular reforms, they were nonetheless concerned about their lack of adequate housing and dining facilities for undergraduates. Like the dilapidated student accommodations in Harvard Yard before its renovation, George Pierson described Yale's dormitories as "mere city barracks." The housing situation was remedied partially in 1920 with the completion of the Memorial Quadrangle, a residential complex funded by the Harkness family, which provided housing and meals for over six hundred students. But even with the addition of the quadrangle, three hundred to four hundred freshmen had nothing in the way of organized college living or dining.[23]

Along with inadequate housing, the indifference of a large number of Yale students toward academic values also resembled conditions at Harvard. Once described by Edwin Slosson as a "likable lot of fellows," Yalies were generally observed to possess better social than intellectual instincts. The prevailing social standards at Yale College stressed gentlemanliness and achievement in campus activities, and undervalued academic success.[24] As at Harvard, exclusive student organizations dominated campus social life. The most prominent were the three senior societies, the junior fraternities, and the Sheffield Scientific School societies.

Although Yale may have lacked interest in the methods of Oxbridge, the physical transformation of the campus that took place in the early decades of the twentieth century tied Yale unmistakably with English culture. Under the direction of architect James Gamble Rogers, a construction program of new buildings made Yale over in the Gothic Revival style. In Harkness Quadrangle, Sterling Library, and several other buildings constructed in the 1920, Rogers embellished the Gothic style with architectural and ornamental allusions to Yale's history and cultural heritage. Paul Turner observed that the aim of creating an environment of "collegiate intimacy, clubby good humor, and confirmation of an ancient and noble institutional heritage" was achieved by designs that suggested medieval domestic, defensive, ecclesiastical, and collegiate life, and by an "abundance of memorial tablets, shields, inscriptions, and other carved devices set into the walls and gateways, serving not only to honor financial benefactors of the college, but also to display its history and the accomplishments of its alumni." Henry Seidel Canby reflected that the "Gothic walls seemed to shut off our college competitions from the cruder world outside us, and fostered an illusion of an American utopia. Others, less impressionable than I and more powerful, were infected with a like romance, and poured out millions into brick and stone antiquarianism to realize their ideal."[25]

Even after Harvard and Yale invested significant resources in academic and residential initiatives, the social and intellectual experience of undergraduates at Harvard and Yale — as well as at many other American colleges and universities — was still perceived by many as inadequate. At Harvard, the construction of the freshman halls, the renovation of the Yard, and the elimination of the Gold Coast did not result in the social mixing of undergraduate students that Lowell desired. The wealthiest and most socially elite students remained segregated from the rest of the undergraduates.[26]

Nevertheless, Lowell continued to believe that a common residential experience could unite disparate student populations. Other college leaders shared this opinion. President Kerr D. MacMillan of Wells College in Aurora, New York, for example, wrote in the *Association of American Colleges Bulletin* in 1927 that the answer to the problem of undergraduate alienation was for colleges and universities to establish residential houses of about two hundred students, along with resident deans and some faculty members. MacMillan contended that the chief advantage of this system would be the establishment of esprit de corps: "A body of 200 can be observed, regulated and guided in a way that you cannot now guide individuals scattered all over the campus."[27] Although the proposals of MacMillan and others provided interesting details on how students might be organized and how socialization might take place, they were nonspecific on the nature of interaction between resident faculty and students.

The philanthropic Edward Harkness was among those who decried the social state of affairs, particularly at Yale. His prodigiously wealthy family had a long record of financial support for Yale. His father, Steven V. Harkness, had been a silent partner of John D. Rockefeller in the early days of Standard Oil. An older brother, Charles, greatly expanded the family fortune, enabling Edward to pursue his philanthropic ways.[28]

Harkness's character played a significant role in his interest in creating Oxford-like student residences. He had been shy as an undergraduate and was sympathetic toward those students who were not selected for membership in a fraternity or society. He left college feeling that an education without social rounding was incomplete; he was therefore interested in projects that could provide such an experience for future students of Yale College. Despite all his support for his alma mater, Harkness apparently never developed a deep understanding of the issues that affected Yale's academic life. Yale historian George Pierson noted that Harkness also had a rather outdated view of undergraduate education and held romanticized notions of life in English universities.[29]

In contrast with Harvard's lengthy interest in residential colleges, at Yale the idea became popular only after James Rowland Angell became president in 1921. He was the son of James Burill Angell, president of the University of Michigan, and studied with John Dewey, Charles Peirce, and the German philosopher Friedrich Paulsen. With this background, Angell had much in common with the teutonized research scholar whom men like Lowell often held responsible for the condition of undergraduate education. Angell had been a professor of psychology at the University of Chicago, and, with John Dewey and Harvey Carr, he pioneered the field of functional psychology. Although rooted in the values of research and professional scholarship, Angell was nevertheless sympathetic to the plight of undergraduate students adrift in the university. He was convinced that Yale, under its present conditions, offered many of its students "slender and inadequate opportunity for the development of their personality, and little or no opportunity to make the peculiar and often valuable contribution which they have to offer to our common academic life." Moreover, he maintained, there was "extremely inadequate opportunity for friendly informal contact between students and members of the faculty."[30]

In 1925, Angell proposed the idea of developing residential colleges to the Yale Corporation's Educational Policy Committee. Although Angell was not overly specific about his educational objectives, he believed that establishing a system of student residences modeled after the colleges of Oxbridge could facilitate the orderly expansion of Yale College: "Not the least of the advantages of the plan," he noted, "is that [the residential college idea] offers a solution similar to that which through the centuries Oxford and Cambridge have found so invaluable for dealing with the pressure to expand."[31]

Although most of the corporation members were more intrigued by than supportive of the idea, one trustee, Samuel Fisher, was interested enough to solicit the financial support of Edward Harkness. Harkness was skeptical at first but was not uninterested; he suggested that Fisher also solicit the opinion of his friend James Gamble Rogers. Rogers had initial reservations about the plan but felt, like many alumni of his day, that something needed to be done to revive the "old-time college spirit" at Yale. He was reportedly won over to the residential college idea when he met a Yale undergraduate unfamiliar with the names of the freshman crew team.[32]

In the summer of 1926, Harkness acceded to the influence of Fisher and Rogers and decided to support the plan. He offered Angell funding for several residential colleges on the condition that the benefaction remain anonymous. Accepting the offer and developing a workable plan, however, posed political problems for Angell more serious than Harkness had anticipated. The undergraduate component of Yale University then consisted of two distinct entities, Yale College and the Sheffield School, each with its own governing board. Any plan to divide Yale undergraduates into an even greater number of academic entities might exacerbate existing political differences and be seriously challenged by various interest groups. Additionally, Yale was in the midst of a capital campaign, and Angell worried that news of a very large gift might forestall contributions from other donors.[33]

Nevertheless, Angell continued to explore the idea. In March 1927, Angell, Fisher, and Rogers traveled to England to visit

Oxford, Cambridge, and several other universities. Fisher and Rogers were impressed with how the residential colleges appeared to facilitate student social life. But Angell took a more skeptical stance and contemplated a broader educational mission for the colleges. He spent more time than his colleagues in observing the interplay between student and don, and he was struck by the degree of separation that characterized this relationship. He returned from his Oxford visit critical of the notion that creating interaction between student and faculty was as simple as having these groups live and dine together. His reservations about what he had seen at Oxford caused him to offer what Pierson called an "illuminating but noncommittal report" on the prospects of implementing residential colleges.[34]

While Angell's skepticism may have delayed the development of the residential college plan, it was not the only stumbling block. Harkness's insistence that the conditions of his offer not be revealed also obstructed progress. In May 1927, two months after his return from England, Angell appointed a faculty committee to study ways to improve student life at Yale. As a result of his enforced silence, Angell could not provide information to the committee that might have helped it produce a proposal that Harkness was likely to approve. In March 1928, ten months after its formation, the committee was nowhere close to the mark. Instead of proposing construction of residential colleges for upperclassmen, the committee was advocating the erection of four freshman quadrangles and additional dormitories for Yale's Sheffield Scientific School.[35]

Harkness was displeased by what he interpreted as a lack of concern for his offer. He told Angell that he would need a response to his offer by July 1, because he wanted to make a similar offer to another institution. Recognizing the nature of the problem, Samuel Fisher suggested to Harkness that providing the committee with information about the bequest might have expedited progress, but Harkness was resolute in his desire to maintain secrecy. In another attempt to break the impasse, James Gamble Rogers approached Yale Provost Charles Seymour and Yale College Dean Clarence Mendell with an idea more likely to meet Harkness's approval. Like Harkness, Rogers was not particularly interested in Oxford's intellectual or pedagogical apparatus, believing instead that the social and cultural advantages of the English system were of primary importance.

In a scheme remarkably similar to one put forward by Lawrence Lowell in 1907, Rogers suggested housing all freshmen in the dormitories of Yale's old campus. After spending their freshman year in common quarters, students would move into one of several residential colleges, which would combine students from both Yale College and the Sheffield School. Seymour was receptive, but Mendell opposed the plan. He thought it would result in the de facto incorporation of the Sheffield student body into Yale College and therefore would not win faculty support.[36]

Little headway had been made by the faculty committee by midsummer, and Harkness was angered by Angell's failure to contact him regarding the plan. In October, when the men did finally speak, Angell was unable to offer Harkness a satisfactory explanation either for the committee's inability to formulate a plan or for his own failure to respond.[37] Ten days later Harkness made good on his intention to interest another institution in the residential college idea and visited Lawrence Lowell at Harvard. During their interview Harkness agreed to provide $3 million to construct an honors residential college, with a master, resident tutors, and students selected from the sophomore, junior, and senior classes. After over three years of seemingly fruitless discussion at Yale, Harkness's offer was accepted by Lawrence Lowell, according to Samuel Eliot Morison, in "about ten seconds."[38] Lowell's ability to capitalize on the moment went even further. After marshaling support for the honors college among faculty and alumni, he persuaded Harkness to provide more than $11 million toward the construction of a system of residential houses. Harkness agreed to fund the construction of three new buildings but stipulated that the remainder of the houses had to be converted from existing structures, including the freshman halls and the former Gold Coast dormitories.[39]

Although there were certainly some at Harvard bound to oppose any measures that might impinge on "Harvard individualism," Lowell was in a better position than Angell to act promptly to accept Harkness's offer. Thanks to the legacy of Charles Eliot's forty-year tenure in office, the Harvard president generally wielded more authority in relation to the faculty than did his counterpart at Yale. Lowell's position was also strengthened by the existence of a 1926 recommendation by Harvard's Student Council that Harvard College be divided into smaller units for social and residential purposes. This report, which suggested that the residential college idea was supported by Harvard's undergraduate student leadership, gave Lowell leverage to counter the potential resistance from club men—both undergraduates and alumni—concerned about the impact of the houses on existing social establishment.[40]

Many of Yale's stalwarts recoiled in surprise when the Harvard plan was announced. In the aftermath, however, Angell regained a place in Harkness's good graces and appointed a committee of administrators and alumni to formulate a residential college proposal to meet all of Harkness's conditions. This committee, which could now operate with full knowledge of Harkness's intentions, drafted a plan for upper-class colleges that explicitly dropped any references to honors work, tutorial instruction, or any other curricular connections to which the benefactor might object. At his own expense Rogers drew up a portfolio of architectural plans. Yale Corporation endorsed the concept, and within ten days Harkness indicated his probable interest in funding Yale's residential college plan. On January 3, 1930, after almost four years of frustration and lack of progress, Harkness offered $15.7 million to Yale for the construction of eight residential colleges.[41]

Construction of new facilities and conversion of existing dormitories began at Harvard in 1929. Two houses opened in 1930, and the remaining five opened a year later. Although architect Charles Coolidge and his colleagues retained the Georgian Revival style of the freshman halls, the three new units (Lowell, Eliot, and Dunster) were quadrangular, the rooms looking onto enclosed courtyards in the manner of Oxford colleges. The seven houses collectively accommodated about eighteen hundred students, two-thirds of the upperclassmen. To create a link with the past, the houses were named for men who had played a prominent role in Harvard's history: Dunster, Eliot, Leverett, and Kirkland were named for Harvard presidents; Lowell, Adams, and Winthrop honored families with long traditions of involvement with the university. The houses, clustered near the Charles River, created a new focal point for the campus that rivaled its traditional center, Harvard Yard. To Professor Henry Aaron Yeomans, the view of the Georgian Revival edifices, spires, and numerous chimneys of the houses was comparable in majesty to Oxford's venerable horizon. When Harkness saw the vista from the Charles for the first time he reportedly expressed his regret that Yale, too, was not built along a river.[42]

The Yale colleges, constructed or remodeled between 1930 and 1935, reflected the continuing influence of James Gamble Rogers, who designed seven of the eight original units. As at Harvard, the names of the colleges commemorated Yale's past, though at Yale they tended to emphasize the distant past. Two colleges, Branford and Saybrook, were carved out of Rogers's Gothic Memorial Quadrangle: they were named for the towns in which Yale had been located before its move to New Haven. The rest of the residential colleges were named for famous men once associated with Yale: Berkeley College was named for Bishop George Berkeley, who donated land and books to Yale in the eighteenth century; Calhoun and Jonathan Edwards honored famous Yale alumni; Davenport and Trumbull were named for prominent figures in Connecticut's colonial history, and Pierson commemorated Yale's first president. Although Yale had no river from which to observe a neo-Oxonian skyline, Rogers evoked Wilson's notion of "gardens of the mind" by his skillful use of the quadrangular complexes of buildings arrayed around courtyards. Like the Oxford colleges, these environments created islands of tranquility in the midst of a large city. Six of the residential colleges were executed in variations of the Gothic Style, one in Georgian Revival, and the final one, Davenport, was built with a Gothic exterior facing the street and a Georgian facade facing its courtyard.[43]

The interior layout of both the houses and colleges were patterned largely after the freshman dormitories at Harvard, thus continuing the trend of copying physical features of Oxbridge colleges. The college complexes included common rooms, large elaborate dining halls, and accommodations for resident faculty and masters. Residents of Harvard's houses and Yale's colleges shared suites that included a common sitting room with a fireplace. Harvard, perhaps remembering the flight of students from the Harvard Yard dormitories in the 1880s, also installed bathrooms in each suite; Yale demurred at providing so much plumbing and installed bathrooms on each floor to be shared by several suites.[44]

Concurrent with the construction of the houses and residential colleges, faculty and administrators at Harvard and Yale developed organizational designs to guide life at the residential colleges. Both Lowell and Angell expressed confidence that their residential colleges would provide more than just congenial surroundings for undergraduates. Consistent with their confidence in the educative value of a hybrid English-American university model, the two presidents asserted their belief that the house and residential college plans combined the best aspects of the English college and the American research university. The new living units would provide autonomous and flexible academic and social communities yet remain subject to the ultimate authority of the university. Lowell felt that such control was "no small restraint on selfishness or somnolence." Angell, without leaving aside his belief that the educational advantages of the colleges required more than resident faculty and congenial dining rooms, believed that Yale's colleges could "be so directed and controlled as to avoid the pitfalls which have in England often retarded the fullest and most fruitful development of the university."[45]

Given their intermingled history and common benefactor, it was not surprising that the most distinguishing feature of the Harvard and Yale plans was their similarity to each other. This similarity was evidenced by the physical structures of the houses and residential colleges, the organization and staffing by resident faculty, and the expectation that the new arrangement would provide a coherent life for students while bridging the gap between undergraduate and scholar. Both plans used the residential colleges to emulate three aspects of English university life: First, the colleges would involve the majority of undergraduate students in a coherent student social life. Each unit would develop an identity and personality but not to the point of subverting academic purposes. Second, the houses would facilitate close ties between students and teachers, patterned after a somewhat idealized relationship between don and students. This goal was occasionally expanded to include basing formal instruction in the residential colleges. Third, new residential colleges would be built to help accommodate expanding enrollments rather than simply making the existing colleges bigger.

The chief difference between the two plans was that Harvard's houses were seen as components in a larger attempt to adapt features of Oxford's educational scheme, while the residential colleges represented the totality of Yale's efforts to emulate the practices of English higher education. Both institutions paid far more attention to the development of the residential colleges as social rather than intellectual entities. The relative weight of social and academic considerations was illustrated clearly by the emphasis on devising student selection and distribution processes, and the lack of detailed plans for connecting faculty with students. In spite of Angell's doubts about the spontaneous generation of student-faculty colloquy, invoking a community of ideas within the residential colleges was generally assumed to require little more than placing students and faculty in proximity to one another.

Harvard planned for each house to contain between 200 and 280 students. A master, usually a senior member of the faculty chosen on the basis of his interest in working with undergraduates, presided over the residents and lived in a suite close by or within the House. After 1952 the master was assisted by a senior tutor, another resident faculty member who served as the house's dean of students. Besides the master and senior tutor, about six tutors, who were normally graduate students, also lived in the house. To supplement the resident supervisory staff, faculty members were affiliated with each house. These "associates" were to visit periodically to spend time with the undergraduates.[46]

Harvard staffed the original houses with a strong contingent of academics with an English connection. Two of the seven masters initially appointed were graduates of Balliol College; four of seven senior tutors were Rhodes Scholars; six of about forty-two resident tutors and nine nonresident tutors were Oxonians or Rhodes Scholars. Eight house associates, including Alfred North Whitehead and Samuel Eliot Morison, were educated or taught at Oxford.[47]

The Yale plan was drawn along largely the same lines as the Harvard plan, but the residential colleges were smaller than their Harvard counterparts, averaging about 150 members each. Yale also hoped to recruit distinguished outsiders to serve as college leaders rather than draw from the ranks of current faculty. Yale forthrightly looked to the personal characteristics of the master to spark the chemistry between scholar and student. In language redolent of Woodrow Wilson's description of a preceptor, Angell anticipated that the masters would be "men of fine and commanding personality, possessed of a real flair for intellectual companionship with youth, men who are in the truest sense of the term natural teachers and who will be able to exploit the extraordinary opportunities offered by the life of the quadrangle for helpful and stimulating comradeship with the students in the group."[48]

Both Harvard and Yale appointed masters to an unlimited term. At Yale, the masters were also appointed to professorial rank (if they were not already on the faculty) and were given a generous salary and expense allowance, provided for by an endowment as part of Harkness's gift. Yale's initial complement of masters also included men connected to English universities. Alan Valentine, a Rhodes Scholar who served under Frank Aydelotte at Swarthmore as dean of men, Arnold Whitridge, a grandson of Matthew Arnold, and Charles Seymour, a graduate of King's College, Cambridge, were among the first group. The colleges also had a complement of resident and nonresident "fellows," somewhat analogous to Harvard's tutors but without the expectation that they would perform a curricular function within the colleges. In the interests of attracting an academic cross section of the student body within each college, the fellows were to be drawn from a variety of disciplines.[49]

These plans also sparked considerable criticism from adherents to the old social system and from observers skeptical of the prospects for success. Continuing the tradition of Albert Bushnell Hart and William Roscoe Thayer, critics vocally opposed Oxfordization at Harvard in the late 1920s and early 1930s. In reaction to the adoption of the house plan, H. P. Perkins pointed to the significant differences between the English and American systems of education as obstacles likely to prevent the houses from playing educationally important roles. Perkins drew attention to the specialized nature of academic study at Oxford and to the role of the English public school in providing the general education associated in the United States with the undergraduate college experience. Alumnus David Demarest Lloyd was equally critical of the American interpretation of the English pattern of residential colleges. Lloyd opposed Lowell's assertion that university control was an improvement over the English system, suggesting that more autonomy and a separate endowment would be necessary to make the houses viable academic and social units.[50]

Likewise, not all Yale students were enthusiastic about the plan. Many had allegiances to the old social system, and labeled the new colleges "silk lined kennels." Others criticized the quadrangle plan as pandering to English cultural ideas. Writing in the *Harkness Hoot,* a student humor magazine, William Harlan Hale described Yale as having "jealous visions of the culture of Oxford." "The English University's cult of the gentleman," Hale argued, "has invaded Yale and Harvard, both of which proclaim themselves as primary adherents to the ideal of the scholar." However, Hale himself revealed something of an Anglophilic sensibility when he suggested that his alma mater's quadrangle plan was an attempt to "ape the natural evolution of seven centuries at Oxford by a revolution of seven years at Yale. It is a wish to give modern colleges a varnish of that ivied loftiness and social sanctity native to the ancient English institutions. It is akin to the average American's abject obeisance to visiting European royalty, or to the midwestern grocery salesman's urge to be a Knight Templar." If the characterizations in Milton White's 1936 novel *A Yale Man* were accurate, most students were probably uncertain what the new college system meant. In the novel, the freshman protagonist, unsure of which residential college to select, opts to live in Saybrook because its ivy-covered walls offered a convenient source of vegetation for his guppy bowl.[51]

Harvard and Yale developed elaborate plans for the social aspects of the residential colleges. Consistent with their desire to provide a more accessible social life for undergraduate students, planners worked to ensure that the residential units would not replicate the existing exclusionary social systems. The residential college populations were to be cross sections of the student bodies, mixing pupils of different economic backgrounds, academic interests, and religious affiliations. Harvard continued to exclude African-Americans, and both universities placed informal quotas on Jewish students. At the same time, the residential colleges intended to homogenize the rest of the undergraduate student body. Planners were optimistic that each residential college would, after the Oxbridge pattern, develop its own distinct personality, or, in Newman's terms, a genius loci.

Lawrence Lowell had been concerned with the selection process of house residents for more than two decades. After the demise of the Princeton quadrangle plan, Lowell asked Woodrow Wilson for his advice on how to assign students to residential colleges. Wilson, who shared Lowell's concern with the social mixing of undergraduates, believed that students should be assigned to a quadrangle by the university. Lowell was sympathetic to Wilson's desire to break up social cliques, but he was concerned that students who were faced with entering a residential college with few friends might opt to leave Harvard.

Lowell's alternative to prescribed assignments was to house the entire freshman class in the dormitories in Harvard Yard. Toward the end of their first academic year, students could then apply for membership in a house. But as there was only room for two-thirds of the freshman class, and, since Lowell wished to exclude those who were socially "undesirable," house assignment was not compulsory. On their applications, freshmen were instructed to rank the houses in order of their preference. The masters would then select new members from these applications. In the years following the inception of the house plan, several masters became meticulous about the way they cultivated their student bodies.[52]

There was also concern at Yale for ensuring a cross section of students in each of the colleges, although the racial and ethnic overtones were less overt than at Harvard. Yale's residential college planners agreed with their Harvard counterparts that prescribed housing assignments were undesirable. They wished to maintain an element of student choice, but they believed that without some form of prescription the residential colleges would become stratified according to existing social divisions. As a result, Yale developed a system whereby masters chose a limited number of students. An allocations committee then filled the remainder of the places within each college, based on student preferences. The overall structure of the plan solidified by the mid-1930s, and mirrored many of the ideas put forward by James Gamble Rogers and Lawrence Lowell. All freshmen were required to live in the dormitories on Yale's Old Campus.

At the end of that year they were assigned to a college, membership in which lasted the duration of their undergraduate study.[53]

In some respects the houses and residential colleges markedly changed student life at Harvard and Yale. The concentration of the majority of the undergraduate student bodies into residential environments enabled the houses and residential colleges to provide a critical mass of participants for campus activities. Participation in social life became accessible to many more students than in the old establishment of clubs, societies, and fraternities. Observers generally heralded the social successes of the house and college plans. In 1937, Mowat G. Fraser, a former Rhodesman from Merton College, even described the Harvard-Yale model as a proven arrangement for combining residential and intellectual development. A few years later, the President and Fellows Report of 1949 noted that the house plan facilitated Harvard being a "real college in the English sense of the word—a society of scholars and tutors living together in studies, at meals, in chambers, at prayer, in recreation." In 1942, Archibald MacLeish expressed his satisfaction with the house system; it had replaced the loneliness of Harvard "individualism" with a socially coherent student life that included broadly based association on intellectual interests.[54]

However successful the new systems were in involving more students in college social life, undergraduate social sensibilities did not necessarily change to reflect the new ethos of broader social inclusiveness. In the 1930s and '40s, Harvard and Yale students were still generally more concerned with their social milieu than with the world of ideas. They responded to the new systems by creating their own social hierarchies that assigned relative status to the houses and residential colleges. At Harvard, membership in the houses constructed with Harkness money (Eliot, Lowell, and Dunster) was more prestigious than membership in those converted from existing dormitories. And while the selection procedures limited the numbers of Jews and African-Americans admitted, some of the people whom the houses were designed to attract were not particularly obliging. In the early 1930s the elite preparatory school contingent, known as the St. Grottlesex Crowd (alumni of Groton, St. Mark's, St. Paul's, St. George's Middlesex, Kent, and other northeastern preparatory schools) shunned the houses. Club members also tended to desert the system if Harvard denied their first choice, which was most often Eliot House. In response, Lowell noted unhappily that "already the houses are being classified with the likely result that some of our most 'fashionable' and successful students will refuse to enter the Houses at all unless they gain admission to one of the two or three 'socially eminent ones.'"[55]

Yale's compulsory membership policies for residential colleges had a more immediate impact on the social structure of undergraduate life, but they did not erase the social distinctions within the student body. A requirement that all undergraduate students take at least ten meals per week in their colleges or dormitories dealt a blow to the dining operations of the junior fraternities, who depended on their grills for a large portion of their income. By 1937, all but one of the junior fraternities and all the Sheffield societies were defunct, though the senior societies survived.[56] But as the Yale's old social system declined, the residential colleges increasingly acquired reputations for being either socially desirable or undesirable, and, as at Harvard, were placed into a hierarchy of social desirability. In addition to the undergraduate preference for popular colleges, this process was abetted in some instances by overzealous masters eager to increase the social prestige of their colleges. The most desirable colleges were those that attracted the higher numbers of socially elite students, including the "white shoe" prep school alumni; lesser houses had reputations for being more academic.[57]

Harvard and Yale addressed these issues in different ways. In March 1933, Lowell appointed a committee with himself as chair to revise the selection apparatus. The committee developed an appointment system that attempted to balance each house regarding race (reflecting Lowell's desire to limit the number of Jews), scholastic rank, and private or public school affiliation. Students expressed a rank-ordered preference for three houses; a selection committee then made assignments with quotas for the different student "types." In 1945, Harvard made membership in a house compulsory and initial assignment to a house permanent, thus incorporating nonresident students into the system and eliminating the tendency for students who were unhappy with their first assignment to reapply the following year to a different college.[58]

Following World War II, the emergence of new concerns regarding higher education supplanted the importance of fostering an atmosphere of gentlemanly democracy at Harvard and Yale. As the mass expansion of systems of higher education accompanied the influx of veterans to college campuses, the image of genteel cultivation of intellect around the dining room table became less important than the issues of access and the development of more specialized academic programs. Reflecting these new priorities, Yale, as a result of the initiative of several masters, in 1955 replaced the old method of college assignments with a lottery system that randomly assigned students to a residential college. Although the new system helped to diminish the lingering social distinctions within the colleges, it also ensured that no college reputation could become anything more than ephemeral. As Thomas Bergin, master of Timothy Dwight College in the 1950s, observed, the desire of each college to achieve an identifiable character was, "in the ultimate sense, doomed to frustration" by the new assignment method.[59]

At Harvard, the cross-sectional system established in 1933

was generally regarded as working better than Yale's assignment plan. But, as at Yale, the triumph of the cross-sectioning philosophy also undid the ability of houses to develop discernible identities. Like Bergin, sociologists Christopher Jencks and David Riesman found that prescribed assignments and cross-sectioning precluded the emergence of distinct house identities. Jencks and Riesman also suggested that, even after the marked increase in the academic caliber of the Harvard College student body in the 1950s and '60s, increased efforts to create stable and enduring identities for the houses would in all likelihood revive the social typing of the early 1930s. They noted that in an academically competitive institution such as Harvard, students would likely create rigidly nonacademic cultures based on society, culture, athletics, or friendship rather than on academic or intellectual values.[60]

The development of the residential colleges' educational roles proceeded with less intensity and less direction than did the management of their social aspects. At neither Harvard nor Yale did the residential college become an integral part of the undergraduate curriculum. At Harvard, the houses were interwoven with the tutorial system, but the predominance of graduate students in tutorial positions meant that the opportunity for student-faculty relationships to develop within the houses fell short of original expectations. Likewise, efforts to teach regular classes within the houses were also limited. At Yale, the absence of a tutorial system, as well as Harkness's insistence on the primacy of the colleges' social function, resulted in less ambitious plans for tying the Yale colleges to the curriculum. Between 1930 and 1970 efforts to create a more formal role for the colleges within the framework of the curriculum were also limited in scope and somewhat sporadic.

The interconnection of Harvard's houses and the tutorial system again revealed the disparities of the quality and nature of tutoring between academic departments. Reflecting problems present in the tutorial system from its inception, graduate students—not faculty—held most of the tutorial positions. Many of the graduate students were drawn to tutorial positions in the houses because such jobs were important sources of financial aid. Besides the fact that students rarely regarded their meetings with tutors as the central focus of their academic work, there were often too few qualified tutors to provide adequate service to the student body. Mirroring the difficulty of departments in sustaining faculty interest in tutorial instruction, the job of house tutor was also typically performed by graduate students, who were only rarely supplemented by professors.[61] In 1975, David Riesman noted that the houses were successful only in creating social and intellectual interaction between faculty and the minority of academically serious students. The interaction "made a difference to those who needed adults to support their academic and intellectual aspirations, since such support was not always forthcoming from peers." For the majority of students, the intellectual possibilities of the houses were not central to their concerns. Along with Christopher Jencks, Riesman concluded that, while the houses provided loci for student life at Harvard, they had not created a "community in which ideas belong primarily to people rather than to the classroom and library." However, Riesman did assert that conclusions regarding success or failure needed to be couched in relative terms: "How one assesses the degree of faculty involvement in the Houses, or indeed the vitality of the House system, depends on one's perspective. If one compares Harvard with most public or private universities, one might conclude that undergraduates are served in the Houses by arrangements which go far beyond the ordinary dormitory complex. . . . If one compares Harvard, however, with Yale, or with superb undergraduate colleges . . . Harvard's senior faculty are much less involved with undergraduate teaching and culture."[62]

Beyond the tutorial system, efforts to integrate the houses and curriculum were sporadic and hampered by lack of enthusiasm on the part of academic departments. In the 1960s there was some revival of interest in house-based instruction. At that time Dean Ernest May of Harvard College solicited the houses to submit ideas for curricular reform, which resulted in the development of a number of experimental courses. After excitement over experimental education faded in the early 1970s it became increasingly difficult to get such courses approved, especially if they were student-directed.[63]

Even before the completion of Yale's first residential college, Edward Harkness's lack of interest in the academic potential of the project portended difficulty in reconciling students' intellectual and social lives in the new living arrangements. Indeed, the spatial arrangements within the residential colleges reflected the primary concern with social rather than intellectual considerations. The colleges did not have classrooms, sufficient library space, or adequate space for seminars or group tutorials. At the same time, however, students enjoyed maid service, security guards, and other appurtenances of gracious living. The lack of accommodation for even rudimentary instructional activity disappointed some of the masters, including Robert Dudley French and Alan Valentine, who expected their colleges to play a larger educational role. Likewise, many of the fellows had anticipated involvement in an adaptation of the English tutorial system. Two masters did set up courses within their colleges, but this practice ceased in 1935 when Harkness discovered that the funds for the courses had come from the masters' entertainment allowance.[64]

The resurgent emphasis on academic concerns following

World War II was clearly evidenced by Yale President A. Whitney Griswold's attempts to rekindle interest in a more formal academic role for the residential colleges. In 1952 a grant enabled Yale to establish within each college three discussion courses of ten students each, called Sophomore Seminars. Resident faculty taught these courses, which were offered within the college. But compared with the concept of an educational center espoused by Angell and like-minded masters and fellows, providing instruction for thirty students per year was a modest step. Thomas G. Bergin, master of Timothy Dwight College from 1953 to 1968, shared this opinion. He noted that "barring revolutionary reordering of the university, the Colleges can never hope to be autonomous or even significant educational centers."[65]

There is no doubt that the residential college plans at Harvard and Yale played a major role in the creation of a residential undergraduate experience in what had become essentially non-residential universities. It is just as clear, however, that efforts to create an intellectual community along the lines of how proponents perceived the Oxbridge residential college fell short of expectations. Several factors contributed to this lack of success.

First, there was no consensus on how the Harvard houses and Yale residential colleges might foster the development of such communities. Edward Harkness and James Gamble Rogers saw Oxford's colleges primarily as picturesque social communities of students. They admired the distinct identities of the English colleges and the loyalty they drew from their alumni. This overriding concern with social considerations was probably influenced by the fact that they were not educators by profession and had little interest in the education programs of the colleges. On the other hand, Lawrence Lowell, like his friend Woodrow Wilson, had more definite ideas on the purposes of the residential college, and more faith in its power to transform the American university. Beyond providing congenial surroundings and esprit de corps, Lowell envisioned the colleges as communities in which older men on the faculty could impart a spirit of intellectual inquiry in a way not possible in a lecture hall. Additionally, Lowell saw the residential colleges as vehicles for the creation of an intellectual and a social elite among those whom he considered to be assimilable into the American common culture. James R. Angell was more skeptical about the residential colleges' ability to generate spontaneous colloquy between student and teacher, but he saw the college as an agent of orderly expansion as the residential system grew.

In spite of this lack of consensus, the attention paid to social considerations consistently outweighed efforts to integrate the colleges into the university's intellectual mainstream. Harvard and Yale went to great lengths over the years to realize the social objectives of the residential colleges. While Harkness's own preferences toward student life issues certainly affected these efforts, the emphasis also reflected some of the realities of university governance. The opposition of proponents of the old social order could be overcome with diligence on the part of the administration, along with Harkness's millions. On the other hand, efforts to reorient the academic culture of the university to suit the requirements of the residential colleges would certainly have invited resistance from faculty and were probably beyond the capability of even a president as powerful as Lowell. As a result, the lack of faculty involvement in the residential college tutorial programs did not lead to change in the faculty reward system to encourage participation. Instead, it simply crippled the program.

The inability to create and sustain distinctive identities for the colleges while forging a common Harvard or Yale identity was another problem. Just as forces in English society outside the universities largely determined the social functions of the Oxbridge college, the creation of the residential college systems at Harvard and Yale did not eliminate entirely the social systems that existed prior to 1929. Indeed, the notion of esprit de corps crucial to residential college proponents in the late 1920s was so intimately associated with the anti-academic forms of student culture prevalent before the houses and colleges were built that it could not be maintained.

Finally, the college systems did not become orderly agents of expansion. Although Angell was the chief proponent of this position and was more discerning than Lowell or Wilson about the spontaneous generation of intellectual contact between student and scholar within the college, his ideas about expanding the network of colleges as the university grew were not well founded. If there was any lesson to draw from Oxbridge regarding expansion, it was that institutional growth had little historical connection with planning. College foundings at Oxford and Cambridge had occurred as the result of the benefactions of individuals without any coordination per se from the universities. Expansion in enrollment was not accommodated by the creation of new colleges.

In practice, institutional growth hurt the residential colleges. Harvard and Yale did not react to the growth in enrollment in the 1940s and 1950s by building more residential colleges. Instead, they crammed more students into the existing colleges, often accommodating undergraduates in rooms intended for resident faculty.[66] Given the expense involved in constructing new facilities, the ever-present competition from other institutional programs, and the uncertainty of private funding, the notion of adding residential colleges in an orderly way was overly optimistic. Harvard and Yale constructed new residential college facilities only after overcrowding made expansion a necessity. After the 1930s, Yale's residential college system only expanded once. In 1962, after several years of intense effort to raise funding, Ezra Stiles and Morse Colleges opened. Harvard's record was somewhat better. Two houses were added in the 1950s, one of which was a nonresidential facility intended for commuters.[67] In 1961, Radcliffe College's dormitories were consolidated into an additional two houses, both of which became coeducational in 1971. Another two houses were added after 1970, bringing the total to thirteen.

Since the 1930s, the colleges and houses have served as centers of undergraduate residential and social life, and their physical presence, true to Ralph Cram's tenets, adds much to the ambience of the two campuses. Despite the expectations of their so many of framers, the houses and residential colleges failed to create a superior hybrid of the English and American varieties of higher education.

5

Claremont

Burton Clark observed that the self-image of American colleges and universities has often been grounded in an institutional *saga*, a collective understanding of institutional character that centers on an emotionally embellished account of a particular school's past. Often that saga has included an account of how a heroic leader struggled against the odds to lead the school to the distinctive position it now enjoys. The hero of the Claremont Colleges saga is undoubtedly its founder and first president, James Blaisdell, but the story of Blaisdell's plan to create an Oxford-like federation of colleges in southern California did not end in the realization of his vision. Instead, the development of the Claremont Colleges illustrated how issues confronting American colleges in the twentieth century led to the abandonment of the major tenets of his plans. Despite Blaisdell's half-century presence at the Claremont Colleges, the president's colleagues opted to move further into the mainstream of American higher educational institutional governance at almost every critical juncture. What began as the "Oxford of the Pacific" developed into what Alexander Astin described in 1967 as a "precarious balance between separate homogeneous entities that resemble the multiversity, and a collection of completely homogeneous, "faceless" liberal arts colleges."[1]

In the early 1920s, Blaisdell, president of Pomona College, committed himself to converting his institution into an Oxford-like cluster of small colleges. His ideas were similar to those that James R. Angell and Lawrence Lowell used to support their residential college plans. Blaisdell hoped that a system of residential colleges would help to maintain intellectual and personal closeness between undergraduates and faculty even as Pomona grew in size. Despite the similar approach, the circumstances at Pomona were markedly different from those at Harvard or Yale. The eastern institutions embraced the college idea to help narrow the rift between undergraduate students and faculty, whose ever-increasing distance from one another was blamed on the size and unitary organization of the research university. In contrast, the adoption of the "Group Plan" at Pomona was aimed at preventing the emergence of such a structure. In 1927, George Santayana remarked that the Harvard house plan might have been more successful had it been undertaken twenty years earlier, before Harvard's transformation into a research university.[2] Blaisdell believed that Pomona College was still young enough — and organizationally pliant enough — to effect the creation of a community of small colleges.

Pomona College, one of the first institutions of higher learning in southern California, was founded by the Congregational Church in 1887 to provide coeducational instruction in the liberal arts. Growth at Pomona College, like that at several other small liberal arts colleges in the region, was stimulated by the state's failure to provide a public institution of higher education for southern California.[3] Although the college was originally situated in the town of Pomona, in 1888 it moved to Claremont, the site of a largely undeveloped planned community five miles to the northeast. This move was the result of an arrangement between Claremont's principal developer, the Pacific Land Improvement Company, and the board of trustees at Pomona College. The real estate market in the Pomona Valley had soured, creating financial trouble for the Pacific Land Improvement Company, whose holdings in Claremont rapidly lost value. To minimize losses, four of the company's directors, including Pomona Trustee Chairman H. A. Palmer, offered to donate an unfinished hotel and 260 additional lots of real estate to the college. In exchange, the college was to sell off lots at its discretion until it generated $5,000 to repay the directors. The plan was attractive to both the developers and the college: Pomona College received assets and real estate, while the establishment of a college in Claremont provided a focal point to the community and promised to revive prospects for growth.[4]

The relocation of Pomona College to Claremont aided town and gown. The college prospered while the surrounding development flourished. During the first two decades of the twentieth century, Pomona's enrollment kept pace with the rapid expansion of the greater Los Angeles area. Between 1900 and 1910, the population of Los Angeles County increased from about 170,000 to more than 500,000. Pomona's student body climbed to over 500 by 1910; by 1916 it had reached almost 600 and was continuing to grow.[5]

While this increase boded well for the economic well-being of the college, the trustees were concerned that the growth might impair the college's ability to maintain its strong undergraduate emphasis. They, along with Blaisdell, were not comfortable with the idea of Pomona College developing into a research university similar to northern California's Stanford University. These concerns coincided with contemporary excoriations about "bigness" made by administrators and faculty at such institutions as Harvard and Chicago. In 1919 the board voted to cap Pomona's enrollment at 700 students, although a few months later it upped the number to 750.[6]

Blaisdell became Pomona's president in 1910. Before assuming this office he was professor of biblical literature and college librarian at Beloit College in Beloit, Wisconsin. He was a solid member of the vocal minority of educators not favorably moved by German influences on American higher education. Blaisdell felt that German influence created divisions that ran "athwart [the] course" of the modern college. Rather, he admired Oxford, particularly Balliol College, which he considered the most distinguished college in the world.[7] He hoped that "instead of one great undifferentiated university," Pomona might develop into a "group of institutions divided into small colleges—somewhat on the Oxford type." "In this way," he noted, "I hope to preserve the inestimable *personal* values of the small college while securing the resources of a great university."[8]

The campus environment that Blaisdell sought to reform was typical of that of colleges in pre-1920s America. Only a fraction of Pomona's student body lived in dormitories. Prior to 1908, Pomona College possessed only one residence hall, which was reserved for female students. A male dormitory was constructed in 1908, but no other student housing was built on campus for another twenty years. The lack of student accommodations was not, however, a manifestation of Teutonic ambivalence toward the personal lives of students; it simply reflected the financial priorities typical of colleges like Pomona. Dormitories were expensive to build, and modern academic buildings were needed more urgently.[9]

Since little on-campus housing was available, most students boarded in houses in the town of Claremont. Groups of male students typically leased houses, which functioned as loci for social life and served as the headquarters for informal fraternities. Pomona College authorities prohibited female students from organizing Greek-letter societies, however, and imposed additional social and parietal restrictions. Faculty members attempted to regulate student life as best they could, but so long as most student housing was outside of direct college supervision, their power to supervise out-of-classroom time was limited. While these authorities did not move to prohibit the fraternity houses, they did promulgate some membership regulations to which students generally adhered. Several local fraternity chapters were established, but only a few endured to become permanent organizations. Most of these fraternities held their meetings and activities in campus buildings.[10]

Like Lawrence Lowell, Blaisdell was skeptical of the role that fraternities played in campus social life. He felt that the fraternity membership selection was undemocratic and that some students would always be excluded. Consistent with this belief, Blaisdell and the faculty prevented the further expansion of Pomona's fraternity system. College authorities consistently opposed efforts to establish sororities or to allow fraternity chapters to affiliate with national organizations.[11]

Further mirroring Lowell's beliefs about student social life, Blaisdell looked admiringly toward Oxford and its residential colleges. Part of his understanding of Oxford may have come from J. Wells's *Oxford and Oxford Life,* a manual for matriculating Oxonians, first published in 1892. Blaisdell recommended this book as an authoritative source on Oxford to trustee George Marston when the Group Plan was first being developed. *Oxford and Oxford Life* was quite unlike *An American at Oxford.* While Corbin's account presented Oxford as the deus ex machina for his critique on American higher education, Wells's book merely provided practical information for the student about to encounter Oxford for the first time.[12] In theory, the treatment of Wells's book should have provided Blaisdell with a less idealized impression of Oxford than one based on Corbin's book. But judging from Blaisdell's early statements concerning the Group Plan and its resemblance to Oxford, his acquaintance with the *Oxford and Oxford Life* may have been cursory. His discussions of instruction made almost no reference to the tutorial system, and, inexplicably, he concluded that the English classroom was a mainstay of intercollegiate comity.[13]

Some of the discrepancies in Blaisdell's understanding of Oxford may have risen indirectly from his association with Malcolm Wallace, a graduate of the University of Toronto, who was his colleague on the Beloit faculty. Wallace taught English literature there and raised his department to prominence within the college. Beloit President Edward Dwight Eaton described Wallace as "thoroughly modern in method" and a "tonic intellectual influence on the life of the college." In 1904, Wallace left Beloit and joined the faculty of University College at the University of Toronto, but he and Blaisdell remained in contact.[14] In 1922, Blaisdell sent his assistant, Robert J. Bernard, on a fact-finding trip to a number of colleges in the northeastern United States. Most importantly, the trip also included a visit to the University of Toronto.

Like Oxford, the University of Toronto was organized around residential colleges and had a strong reputation for classics and literature. Bernard was intrigued by the collegial structure of the University of Toronto, which he assumed was built on the Oxford plan.[15] This assumption, however, was incorrect. Although the University of Toronto's undergraduate program was indeed based on a network of small colleges with similar curricula, that was the extent of any similarity to Oxford. Toronto had in fact followed an idiosyncratic pattern of development that reflected the political and religious climate of nineteenth- and early-twentieth-century Ontario.

The University of Toronto grew out of Anglican King's College, a province-supported institution founded in 1827 and secularized in 1849. In 1854 an examining agency patterned after the University of London was organized and named the University of Toronto. At the same time, the faculty of King's College was reconstituted as University College. In the manner established by the University of London, University College and the other institutions of higher education in Ontario—

which included several denominational colleges—were to send their graduates to the university for examination before degrees could be confirmed. In practice, only University College ever sent up any students for examination, meaning that in essence University College was the de facto University of Toronto.[16]

Late in the century Toronto followed the lead of American institutions like Johns Hopkins and labored toward developing itself into a modern research university. In the process, the London model was modified greatly; the university again became a teaching body, offering instruction in science, mathematics, and other modern subjects. Only after the University of Toronto became the preeminent university in the province did other institutions opt to confederate. Three of the denominational colleges joined the university before 1900. They maintained their largely classical curricula and religious instruction and relied on the university faculties to provide instruction in other areas. As the university expanded the breadth and depth of its curriculum in modern subjects, the instructional function of the college became less and less important. On the basis of later inquiries Blaisdell made to Wallace, he apparently thought that there was a rational division of instruction between the college teaching staff and the university faculties.[17]

These were not the only differences that should have alerted Blaisdell and Bernard that Toronto was an inappropriate surrogate model for Oxford. First, Toronto was an urban institution and therefore less oriented around the residential experience of students. In 1927, only about 1,000 of its over 2,750 undergraduates were in residence.[18] Second, Toronto lacked a tutorial system; as in American universities, lectures were the most common form of instruction.

Leaving aside his interest in Toronto and his failure to grasp the finer points of English university governance, Blaisdell developed a curricular philosophy that conformed to the Arnoldian ideals that had been popular at Oxford since the mid-1800s. Blaisdell insisted that a college not steer its students toward definite utilitarian objectives but instead provide them with a "deliberate acquaintance with cosmopolitan knowledge and sympathies before entering on the more direct narrowed and intensive training for a life calling."[19] He believed that students' close relationships with college faculty would provide that broad-based education.

In 1925, the year after Bernard's trip, Blaisdell suggested to the Pomona trustees that the future development of Pomona College should follow a "group system" with a central library and laboratories serving several small colleges. Blaisdell viewed this scheme as a "median course . . . between unilateral expansion and staying small." "Instead of one great, undifferentiated university," he asserted, "we might have a group of institutions divided into small colleges.[20] The trustees, especially George Marston, were receptive to this idea, and they commissioned Blaisdell and his staff to develop a preliminary statement for what was to become known as the Group Plan. This statement, completed in 1925, offered Blaisdell's rationale for developing a confederation of small colleges. First, he sought to retain the "intimate and personal relationships between faculty and students" as the institution expanded. Second, he hoped to keep the costs down for expensive facilities, such as libraries and laboratories. Third, he wanted to increase consideration for the importance of living conditions, in which students spend "four plastic years." Fourth, he wanted to develop a physical environment in which architecture projected an impression of "interesting, stimulating and inspiring life."[21]

Blaisdell's proposed adaptation of the Oxford pattern clearly owed more to the organizational pattern of the University of Toronto than of an English university. In place of Oxford's centripetal structure, in which colleges controlled a major portion of the resources and instructional facilities, Blaisdell conceptualized an institution in which the sphere of the college was more limited—that is, closer to the college's profile at Toronto. Claremont Colleges was to be built around distinct components called colleges and academic centers.

The fully developed group would encompass a number of colleges that comprised residential facilities, dining halls, faculty offices, and informal meeting space. The colleges might be single-sex or coeducational, depending on the circumstances of its founding, but Blaisdell did not desire much curricular diversity between colleges. In contrast, the academic centers would consist of libraries, lecture halls, and other facilities related to the courses of study. These might be shared by more than one college, or, like a main library or an auditorium, shared by all of the constituent colleges. In this way the cost of these faculties could be borne collectively and duplication avoided.[22]

The major emphasis of the college was to be social rather than academic. What Blaisdell called the "daily life of the student," the informal contact between student and student and between student and faculty, would serve as the wellspring of the college's intellectual life. The Claremont Colleges, Blaisdell asserted, would become a "place where students not only live but where a definite attempt is made to appropriate this life in terms of the interests of matters intellectual. In other words, the aim is to return to the original English idea of the college where scholars live and think together." By developing the institution in this fashion Blaisdell believed he was capturing the essence of Oxford. "In creating and maintaining their individuality," he noted, the English colleges "have put their reliance on the development and presence of their personal association and intimacy in the residence life rather than on the collegiate segregation of their lecture halls and classrooms." Blaisdell was also convinced of the educational importance of intellectual conversation around the dinner table. He hoped that over time the colleges would develop a "noble competition" with one another, mirroring the athletic rivalries that existed between Oxford's colleges.[23]

Maintaining the smallness of the college was a key element to Blaisdell's plan. He proposed that the colleges remain limited in size—both in enrollment and in physical property. All facilities that were not specifically concerned with the "area of personal relations between the separate college and its students" were to be incorporated into the academic centers. Blaisdell believed that this arrangement would relieve the college presidents of the range of administrative duties that detracted from the maintenance of an academic community.[24]

There were also practical dimensions that enhanced the group plan's attractiveness. California law limited educational institutions to one hundred acres of land allowable as tax exempt; establishing a cluster of independent colleges was therefore more sensible than creating one unitary institution. Blaisdell also thought that the Group Plan would help attract private financial support, since it expanded the number of projects that might interest donors. In the mid-1910s several Pomona trustees began working to urge wealthy, socially prominent southern Californians to support the college.[25]

The Group Plan received national press coverage, and the attention revealed some contradictions in constituents' perceptions of the plan. One question seemed to pervade the literature: Was the Claremont Colleges plan an attempt to copy Oxford or a unique American institutional adaptation? The answer appeared to depend on whom one asked. Claremont constituents relished having their way with both sides of the question. In 1925, E. H. Kennard, Pomona's first Rhodes Scholar, asserted that "no particular detail of [Oxford] is likely to prove satisfactory here if copied outright. Rather, one should study Oxford thoroughly and then, burning his notes, face the problem anew and seek to devise a form of education suitable to America." Agreeing with Kennard was Pomona faculty member George Savage, who wrote in 1927 that "no effort was being made to copy the organization of any other institution but to develop step by step in American terms." On the other hand, Pomona College Trustee President George W. Marston noted proudly in 1931 that the project was indeed the "Oxford Plan of the Pacific." And faculty member N. W. Stephenson acknowledged the importance of Oxbridge in providing direction to Claremont. Responding to the suggestion that the Claremont plan was an attempt to imitate Oxford in American conditions, he replied that "probably there is no one in Claremont who be troubled if you pay our undertaking the high compliment of the implied suggestion. We modestly fall silent. To the extent of trying to learn from the two great English instances of federated university . . . we obviously are seeking to profit by their example."[26]

After the official adoption of the Group Plan in 1925, the Pomona trustees worked toward the establishment of a second college, as well as a corporate entity that would ultimately relate to the group of colleges as Oxford University related to its colleges. This entity, which Blaisdell dubbed Claremont Colleges, was to serve as the development agency of the Group Plan and to coordinate matters of common concern to the colleges, particularly graduate education.

Scripps College for women, the second Claremont College, was founded in 1926. Interest in a single-sex institution demonstrated the sensitivity that founders had for the regional higher education market. At the time, southern California lacked a nondenominational women's college. Much of the financial support for the college came from Ellen Browning Scripps, a wealthy retiree whose fortune came from the newspaper industry. Scripps, who was from England, was very receptive to Blaisdell's notion of bringing some of Oxford's tradition and practice to Southern California.[27]

Scripps's entire architectural and scholastic plans were worked out before construction began, a measure not taken at most existing American colleges, including Pomona College. Reflecting Blaisdell's desire to use architecture to create a "stimulating environment," and consistent with their Oxonian fervor, the trustees chose an English architect, Gordon B. Kaufman, to oversee the design. Kaufman's plan for Scripps contrasted sharply with the arrangement of Pomona College, which, like many colleges founded in the nineteenth century, encompassed a variety of buildings laid out informally within a parklike setting. Scripps clearly showed the influence of the Oxford quadrangle: the buildings were arrayed around the perimeter of an elongated main plaza, and many of the buildings faced on to small square loggias and patios of their own. Walls and gates connected the buildings so that the interior plazas were not visible from outside. In a manner suggesting the architectural ideas of Ralph Adams Cram, Kaufman retained the essence of the English quadrangular layout but substituted a local building style for the Gothic or Colonial Revival architecture favored in the East. Scripps's buildings were based on the Mexican hacienda–influenced architecture prevalent in California in the 1920s.[28]

The incorporation of Claremont Colleges, Blaisdell's equivalent to Oxford's university corporation, was the beginning of a long and confusing trail of events that saw the function and composition of Claremont's "university" change several times. Consistent with his desire to emulate English tradition, Blaisdell insisted that there be no written constitution for the Group Plan, preferring instead to allow precedent to shape the course of the project. Beyond the elemental idea of a board of nine trustees, called "fellows" to distinguish them from Pomona and Scripps board members, the scheme for Claremont Colleges remained vague. It was assumed, however, that a majority of the fellows would be college trustees. Seven of the first nine fellows were also Pomona Trustees, and Blaisdell was elected the first "head fellow." [29]

Blaisdell's acknowledged source of inspiration for the central body was the Oxford University Corporation, but Claremont Colleges' role in graduate education and development, and its lack of an examination function, again placed it more in the mold of Toronto's "university" than Oxford's. Nevertheless, Oxford was still the model in the eyes of Claremont's framers. Board of Fellows member William W. Clary observed that the language Blaisdell used to describe the relationship between Claremont Colleges and the colleges themselves followed closely the wording used to describe the relationship between Oxford and its constituent colleges in the *Oxford University Handbook*. Like the Oxford University Corporation, Claremont Colleges was to be controlled by the colleges. In early discussions, Blaisdell unsuccessfully advanced the idea that college degrees be countersigned by the Claremont Colleges, much in the way that Oxford divided examination and teaching between the university and the college. [30]

Mirroring the course of events at the University of Chicago and Harvard, Claremont's planners examined the English residential college system in a detailed way only after they had committed themselves to imitate it. Not until after the Group Plan was agreed to in principle did Blaisdell undertake any systematic study of Oxford. In late 1925 he traveled to England to see Oxford, stopping en route to see A. Lawrence Lowell at Harvard to discuss his plans. He had corresponded with Lowell about the Group Plan and had received encouragement without specific advice. "You can do this in California," Lowell noted.

"We cannot do this here."[31] Blaisdell was inspired by his visit to Oxford, but it did not result in any alteration or revision of the Group Plan.

Claremont's Oxonian zeitgeist, which peaked in the late 1920s and early 1930s, was best exemplified by Blaisdell's conception of the Group Plan and by the quadrangular design of Scripps. It was the closest that Claremont ever came to resembling Oxford in an organizational sense. After the mid-1930s the Claremont Colleges receded into the mainstream of American higher education. Rather than becoming a group of intimately scaled colleges that shared a central core of common facilities and some notion of common identity, the Claremont Colleges emerged instead, as John Thelin noted, as a cluster of "New England-style" American colleges.[32] Thelin's argument is substantiated in several ways, as subsequent issues concerning size, curricular focus, and the role of the central entity were resolved in favor of growth and specialization rather than by trying to remain true to the spirit of the plan.

One factor that helped to undermine the Oxonian cast of the Group Plan was the ever-changing role of Claremont Colleges, which over time moved further and further from Blaisdell's idea of an Oxford-like university corporation. In 1930, Claremont Colleges underwent its first organizational overhaul. The fellows added a second administrative component to oversee intercollegiate relations and to manage common facilities. The Administrative Council, as the new body was called, comprised the college presidents, one faculty member from each college, and the Claremont Colleges controller. Meanwhile, the Board of Fellows emphasized the development of graduate education, even though this was supposed to be only one of Claremont Colleges' functions. This emphasis gave Claremont Colleges the appearance of a third college (albeit a graduate college) that seemed to compete with the others rather than to reflect their common interests.[33]

These changes prompted Blaisdell to solicit the input of Malcolm Wallace, then principal of the University of Toronto's University College, to help clarify the division of academic work between the colleges and the university corporation in a collegiate university. Blaisdell asked Wallace whether he could recommend anyone in southern California who had experience with a residential college system and could advise Pomona. He also asked Wallace for information on what types of instruction were provided by Toronto's colleges and what was provided by the university. On both counts Wallace was unable to help. First, he knew of no one in southern California who could advise Blaisdell. Second, and importantly, he informed Blaisdell that the University of Toronto was not an exemplar of an Oxford-style collegiate university, explaining that division between collegial and university instruction at Toronto was almost wholly idiosyncratic.[34]

Blaisdell's notion of an unwritten constitution for the group, after the fashion of the British Parliament, also proved untenable. A formal constitutional framework for the Claremont Colleges was developed and completed in 1942. At that time, Pomona and Scripps developed a statement to govern relations between the three administrations. In the process of crafting their relationship, Claremont Colleges, which had been the linchpin of Blaisdell's plan, was again altered in size and in mission. A stronger central agency, the Intercollegiate Council, replaced the Board of Fellows; it oversaw the administration of inter-institutional concerns, including joint budgets, common facilities, and development plans. This board administered the development of common functions and facilities, such the library, maintenance of physical assets, health services, and the auditorium. The group would also approve the affiliation of future colleges. Blaisdell was predictably upset by the enactment of the plan and expressed concern that the alteration of the mission of Claremont Colleges jeopardized the goals of the plan. Further changes occurred in 1944, including changing the corporate name to Claremont College (singular). At this time there was, however, one rather superficial concession to the Oxford idea. E. Wilson Lyon, president of Pomona College and a former Rhodes Scholar, suggested that the headship of the Board of Fellows rotate annually among the college presidents, similar to the way the vice-chancellorship of Oxford rotated. Lyon would later describe this feature of Claremont's governance as one of the key similarities between Claremont and Oxford.[35]

Within the colleges, new developments progressively undermined Blaisdell's Oxonian ideas. First, the Claremont colleges opted for specialization in a manner that Blaisdell might have viewed as contrary to his scheme. Beginning with Scripps, each new college was founded to help complement the existing curricular offerings of the group. Plans for a third college, a men's institution emphasizing the social sciences and preprofessional curricula, were in progress as early as 1927. Contrary to Blaisdell's original notion of curricularly undifferentiated colleges, all of the colleges established under the Group Plan (that is, all except Pomona) were curriculum-specific. Scripps emphasized the humanities and literature; Claremont Men's College, founded in 1946, centered on public affairs and included majors in humanities, science and mathematics, and social sciences; the curriculum of Harvey Mudd College (1955) was based around the physical sciences and engineering; Pitzer College (1963) emphasized the social and behavioral sciences.[36]

Second, the colleges opted for growth at the expense of intimacy. Instead of limiting the size of the colleges to preserve the human scale, as Blaisdell intended, the Claremont Colleges, following the path of other elite American colleges, moved vigorously to expand enrollments. College constituents had an increasingly difficult time understanding Blaisdell's notion that success meant more than the expanding of facilities and enrollments, a problem that William Clary said was exacerbated by Pomona College's large size relative to the other colleges. Part of this difficulty may have been the result of the discrepancy between Blaisdell's notion of a small college (150 to 300 students) and the late-1920s conception of what constituted a small college (800 or so students was not atypical). The difficulty in getting the colleges to buy into an Oxonian notion of smallness became evident to Blaisdell, who as early as 1931 expressed his concern that "if some legitimate limitation of the separate college is not recognized and the university function is not magnified, we shall simply get the extravagance and waste of a group of highly competitive institutions."[37]

Lending truth to LeBaron Briggs's quip that colleges only emphasize the value of smallness as a means to get bigger, the individual Claremont colleges agreed to the principle of smallness but worked toward expanding their enrollments. Likewise, the pattern of overall growth favored increasing the size of existing colleges rather than adding new small foundations. The group attempted to address this issue in 1942 with its agreement to limit enrollment size. Pomona would limit its enrollment to 800 students, Scripps to 225. Claremont Men's College was not included in the 1942 agreement, but it was generally assumed that it would enroll about 300 students.[38]

The agreement did not, however, settle the issue of collegial scope. Pomona College was intent on maintaining and enhancing its reputation as a nationally prominent liberal arts college, and to expanding its enrollment further. As a result of a temporary increase in enrollment to accommodate returning veterans,

Pomona exceeded its enrollment ceiling of 900 students. A conference in 1950 resulted in the raising of enrollment levels, with the understanding that they would be lowered when financial circumstances made such a move possible. Those circumstances never occurred, and the institutions continued to grow. Claremont President William Clary noted that the resolution of the size question permanently altered Blaisdell's idea of building a community of small colleges. In 1970, Clary noted that "[we] have now developed, instead of a group of small Oxford type colleges, a group of larger American type colleges, which are being described as the 'cluster concept.' "[39] In 1959 the enrollment ceilings were again raised. Pomona increased to 1,100 students, Claremont Men's College to 600, Scripps went to 400, and Harvey Mudd, which had had an initial ceiling of 350, was expanded to 400. By 1969, Pomona College had nearly 1,300 students, Scripps was over 525, Claremont Men's College had passed 800, Harvey Mudd had reached 380, and Pitzer enrolled over 650.[40]

By the mid-1950s, little of Blaisdell's Oxford Plan of the Pacific was evident in the structure or operation of the Claremont colleges. Only superficial similarities with Oxford remained, although the institutional saga continued to reflect Oxford's inspirational value to the development of the Claremont plan. Nevertheless, Claremont's federated structure addressed some of the deficits of the modern research university that Blaisdell had sought to correct. Claremont did become a residential institution in which graduate education did not displace the emphasis on undergraduate teaching. Perhaps David Riesman's pronouncement about the relative success of Harvard's House Plan also holds true in the case of the Claremont colleges. Although the Group Plan never fulfilled the expectations of its framer, what did emerge was an improvement over potentially worse alternatives.

Even with its faults taken into consideration, the Claremont Colleges developed in a way that preserved Pomona College's desire to expand into a major seat of scholarship while remaining committed to undergraduate education. The colleges remained small, if only by American standards. In remaining true to the notion of smallness, Claremont's collegiate structure maintained the undergraduate program at the expense of faculty links between colleges. In 1972, Claremont Colleges President Louis Benezet asserted that the subdivided character of the Claremont faculties was the greatest weakness of the system, noting that intercollegiate academic exchange and academic planning were the least developed cooperative mechanism and the federation's most important problem.[41]

6

The University of California, Santa Cruz

"THE CITY ON A HILL"

The development of the University of California's residential college–based campus at Santa Cruz in the mid-1960s resulted from renewed interest in organizing institutions of higher education around small communities of students and faculty. As in the early twentieth century, increases in the size and number of institutions of higher education in the 1950s and 1960s—along with concern over the integrity of undergraduate education in a research-oriented academic environment—prompted educators to explore ways to restore the human scale to undergraduate education. These efforts occurred at institutions of higher education throughout the United States and took a variety of forms.

The efforts at Santa Cruz were the most ambitious. Planners hoped to develop a 27,500-student university organized around 10 professional schools and 15 to 20 residential colleges, each of which would encompass residential and dining facilities for 600 undergraduates. The residential colleges would also include faculty offices, apartments for resident faculty, classrooms, and other academic facilities. These academic units would share a core of university facilities, including libraries and laboratories. In the words of Dean E. McHenry, the founding chancellor, Santa Cruz "was planned from the beginning with bifurcated aspirations: to make a notable contribution to undergraduate education, with built-in safeguards from later dilution; and to lay a firm foundation for graduate and professional endeavors." Had the Santa Cruz campus developed according to its original plans, it would have become the largest university in the world organized around residential colleges, equaling Oxford or Cambridge in the number of colleges but easily surpassing them in enrollment.[1]

The revival in concern for the quality of the undergraduate experience came after fifteen years of sweeping changes in American higher education. Although the expanding number of students had concerned university administrators since the beginning of the twentieth century, the increase in college and university enrollment that followed World War II was unprecedented in its swiftness. Much of this growth arose from Serviceman's Readjustment Act of 1944, more commonly known as the GI Bill, which enabled returning veterans to enroll in American colleges and universities at government expense. Although planners anticipated that many former soldiers would take advantage of the program, the numbers of enrollees surpassed even those optimistic projections. In 1946 alone, more than 1 million veterans enrolled in colleges and universities, almost doubling the size of the American college student population.[2]

Many of these new students were older, more mature, and less concerned with the out-of-class aspects of college life than were the typical college students of previous eras. This change shifted the importance of many issues that had been considered pressing to higher education in the 1930s. The emphasis that educators placed on the social development of students within intimately scaled learning environments temporarily yielded to the more immediate task of providing adequate education for this large and diverse student population. At the same time, Americans no longer viewed higher education as existing primarily for the privileged or for those who aspired to correct social deficits. The arrival of the veterans and the expansion of the 1950s, according to Diane Ravitch, "broke the genteel cocoon in which much of higher education had been wrapped." The notion that higher education served a limited clientele was replaced by a sense that attending college was purposeful for everyone. What John Hardin Best has described as a "middle class sense of urgency" now maintained that college attendance was a social necessity.[3]

Although veteran enrollments had peaked by the early 1950s, college and university attendance continued to grow. The number of students enrolled in degree programs rose from 2.3 million to 3.6 million between 1950 and 1960. Enrollments were expected to rise further in the mid-1960s, when the baby boomers would approach college age. To respond to this anticipated increase in enrollment, state systems of higher education expanded rapidly in the late 1950s and the 1960s. Between 1961 and 1964 alone, 146 colleges and universities were created in the United States.[4]

This expansion also resulted in increasingly larger institutions. The number of campuses with enrollments exceeding 20,000 students grew from 10 in 1947 to 55 in 1968. The primary impetus behind establishing such large campuses was clearly economic necessity. Unlike early-twentieth-century Progressives, the architects of these new systems did not believe in the efficiency of a society built around large social institutions. Rather, they understood that they had to avoid what might be construed as the unwarranted proliferation of academic programs. To Clark Kerr, one of the chief architects of the development of California's state system of higher education in the 1950s and 1960s, the development of large campuses was "an imperative rather than a reasoned choice among alternatives."[5]

Kerr served as chancellor of the University of California's Berkeley campus from 1952 to 1958, when he became president of the University of California. In both of these positions he showed interest in innovations that might help counteract the alienation that he anticipated undergraduate students would feel in such large settings. Kerr noted that many American universities ought more rightly to be called "multiversities," a name that aptly reflected that academic life in large institutions was now organized around many communities and activities, often with little to unite them beyond a common organizational skeleton and source of economic support.[6] The multiplication of academic communities within the university had been long in the making, but the postwar expansion had heightened the sense of fragmentation that educators sensed within large institutions. Kerr's observations illustrated that the multiversity lacked an animating spirit, what John Henry Newman had called the genius loci, the sense of identity and purpose that all institutional constituents might agree upon. "A community, like the medieval communities of masters and students," noted Kerr, "should have common interests; in the multiversity, they are quite varied, even conflicting. A community should have a soul, a single animating principle; the multiversity has several."[7]

At the other end of the spectrum of institutional types was the small college of limited resources, an institution that existed in greater numbers than the large public university. But just as the small college did not become the rallying point for Progressive Era critics of the "teutonized" research university, small, nonelite institutions were not widely touted as alternatives to the multiversity in the 1960s. To the contrary, there was concern that the academic experience offered by many small American colleges was inadequate to the educational needs of contemporary students. Some critics pointed to the obsolescence of the small denominational college to underscore the urgency for creating small environments within large public universities and university systems. In 1966, C. Grey Austen, editor of the *Journal of Higher Education*, suggested that as many as 25 percent of existing institutions of higher education, specifically small colleges, might already be obsolete. They lacked adequate library resources or trained faculty to keep pace with larger and better funded state institutions and with elite private institutions. If those obsolete institutions disappeared, he said, it would be incumbent on large universities to re-create intimacy within their organizational structures or to run the risk of alienating undergraduates from academe.[8]

Following Austen's logic, one of the major avenues advanced for countering the alienating effects of the mulitversity was the creation of smaller, largely self-contained academic and residential units within the framework of a larger university. Between 1959 and 1974, at least twenty-five colleges and universities created what came to be known collectively as cluster colleges.[9] These efforts typically attempted to create small, intimate academically oriented residential environments for select groups of undergraduate students within large universities, such as Wayne State University's Monteith College and the University of Michigan's Residential College.

Like the earlier generation of academics who opposed the teutonization of the curriculum, proponents saw the cluster college as a means to restore unity to the undergraduate curriculum. As academic departments were held chiefly responsible for this development, such educators as Michigan State University President John Hannah and Berkeley's Joseph Tussman advanced the idea that cluster college programs center on interdisciplinary curricula. This idea owed much of its inspiration to earlier attempts to create coherent core curricula at American universities in the 1930s and 1940s. Among the innovators in these efforts were Alexander Meiklejohn, who first pioneered a core curricula while president of Amherst College from 1912–

23; Robert Maynard Hutchins, president of the University of Chicago (1929–51), who, along with Mortimer Adler labored to implement a fully prescribed undergraduate curriculum based on seminal works of western civilization (that is, a "great books" curriculum); and Scott Buchanan and Stringfellow Barr, who left the University of Chicago in 1937 to establish such a curriculum at St. John's College in Annapolis, Maryland.[10]

In 1927, Meiklejohn became director of the ill-fated Experimental College at the University of Wisconsin, which was built around a two-year interdisciplinary program for freshmen and sophomores. In the first year, students devoted themselves to studying multiple aspects of a classical civilization, including its history, literature, economy, and philosophy. In the second year, students repeated the process for a modern civilization. The goal of the curriculum aimed more to develop a broader perspective concerning the workings of society than to instill information systematically. Meiklejohn's program was terminated after five years because of resistance from both academics and students, but his ideas remained influential.[11]

Hutchins's interest in creating a common undergraduate curriculum was shaped largely by his association with Adler, whom he met in 1927. Adler's intellectual talent and wide range of knowledge heightened Hutchins's awareness of the lack of cohesion of his own undergraduate education. Adler's interest in interdisciplinary teaching and research had been influenced by a great books–based survey course he had taken and later taught at Columbia. Soon after he became president of the University of Chicago, Hutchins began to recruit academics sympathetic to the idea of a common curriculum, including Adler. In 1931 the two men instituted and taught a freshman seminar that exposed students to cultural knowledge based on seminal texts. Hutchins himself read many of the books used in the seminar for the first time.[12]

Hutchins explained his educational ideas in a manifesto entitled *Higher Learning in America,* which was published in 1936. He argued that unless students and professors had a common intellectual training, the university could never be more than a series of disparate schools and departments. Agreeing with Newman, and sounding much like the English anti-utilitarians of the nineteenth century, Hutchins insisted that the most useful education was one that cultivated the intellect. To achieve this end, he advocated a common course of study based on books that "through the centuries attained to the dimensions of classics" by virtue of their ability to draw out the "elements of our common human nature."[13]

In the same year Hutchins attempted to institute a single prescribed undergraduate curriculum based on great books at the University of Chicago. However, this attempt met strong resistance from faculty who were not predisposed toward either radical curricular change or Hutchins's autocratic style. After it became clear that a restructuring of the entire curriculum was not in the offing, Hutchins was successful in replacing the University of Chicago's largely elective curriculum with a series of prescribed yearlong courses that integrated divisional subject areas. But his departure from the Chicago presidency in 1951 left the concept of an integrated interdisciplinary curriculum without a champion, and by the late 1950s his efforts were almost entirely undone.[14]

Open conflict with existing institutional commitments to research and specialized education did little to advance the cause of interdisciplinary curricula. However, university politics might not have been solely to blame for failure. In the case of the University of Chicago, Oscar and Mary Handlin contended that such programs were likely ever possible only with a handful of selected and highly motivated students, not with the general population of undergraduates.[15] Likewise, interdisciplinary teaching required faculty members who were motivated to work outside their subject areas and to devote more time to teaching. Given these conditions, it was not surprising that the most far-reaching and enduring of the interdisciplinary projects was undertaken at St. John's College, a small liberal arts institution free of the sorts of institutional adversaries present at Chicago, Wisconsin, or other universities with a strong commitment to research. Two of the faculty members Hutchins recruited to teach at Chicago—Buchanan and Barr—in 1937 became dean and president, respectively, of St. John's College, where they installed a four-year curriculum devoted solely to the great books approach.

Buchanan, the major theoretician of the St. John's curriculum, was an undergraduate at Amherst College during the Meiklejohn presidency. In 1919 he went to Balliol College, Oxford, as a Rhodes Scholar, where he wrongly assumed that Balliol's relation with the India Civil Service meant that he might study Indian culture and Sanskrit. Buchanan found instead that the college's offerings in that area were virtually nonexistent. He then read philosophy under Balliol's future master, A. D. Lindsay, whose instructional style had a major impact on Buchanan's thinking. Lindsay, according to Buchanan, was adroit in turning almost any issue into a moral question, an approach that became a central feature of great books instruction at St. John's. Barr, who was also a Rhodes Scholar, was a long-time associate of Buchanan's, having served with him on the faculty at the University of Virginia before joining the University of Chicago. Consistent with its prescribed curriculum based on one hundred or so great books, St. John's had no academic departments, majors, or electives, and faculty were not expected to be involved in original scholarly research.[16]

In addition to the influence of great books proponents, much of the impetus behind the cluster college projects came from educators who still looked to the English collegiate university for inspiration. Some of these advocates had direct ties to earlier efforts to emulate the organization of Oxford and Cambridge. Kerr, for one, held an interest in residential colleges that dated back to his undergraduate days as an undergraduate at Swarthmore College during Frank Aydelotte's presidency. In contrast to his sardonic lament over the tripartite reward system of the multiversity—"sex for the students, parking for the faculty, and football for the alumni"—Kerr continued to believe that, as far as undergraduate education was concerned, "any university could aim no higher than to be as British as possible." Likewise, Dean McHenry, who in 1961 became Santa Cruz's first chancellor, had longstanding admiration for the colleges of Oxford and Cambridge. McHenry looked to Newman and the English universities as "beacon lights for undergraduate liberal arts programs," but he acknowledged that at times he viewed the merits of the Oxford colleges somewhat overcredulously because many of the Oxonians he knew seemed extraordinarily well educated.[17] The comments of Warren Bryan Martin, of the University of California's Center for Research and Development in Higher Education, also revealed the sense of enduring respect that existed for Oxbridge:

> A . . . characteristic shared by cluster colleges . . . is a residential arrangement in which facilities and programs combine to keep the student in the climate of learning. Faculty studies, seminar and class rooms, even faculty apartments, or often in or near dorms, Oxford and Cambridge style, to encourage vital academic relationships, and to aid in the achievements of the community. The planners believe, with Aristotle, that the happiness of man is best attained in the life of the community. So, all-

college activities such as "High Table" and "College Night" are held, not only to enhance the academic and aesthetic life, but also to encourage a community by bringing college personnel together in a shared enterprise.[18]

The advocates of cluster colleges also recognized as a major source of inspiration the contributions of earlier efforts to create residential colleges in America. McHenry was a lifelong admirer of Woodrow Wilson and was keenly interested in James Blaisdell's original plan at Claremont. Respect for Claremont was seen elsewhere as well. In 1966 a national conference held to discuss the cluster college concept added the Claremont model to Oxford and Cambridge as an exemplar of a model for cluster college development.[19]

Although many cluster college advocates identified strongly with the residential colleges of Oxbridge and their American imitators, the projects of the 1960s reflected many of the changes that had occurred in American higher education since Harvard, Yale, and Claremont took to the idea in the late 1920s. A key point of departure from earlier thought was that concern for the social life of students was now very clearly linked to the world of ideas. The voices of men like James Gamble Rogers and Edward Harkness, who were primarily concerned with the development of student social life, were not heard among the new generation of proponents. The notions of the "clubby democracy" of Lawrence Lowell or the unself-conscious elitism of Matthew Arnold were also absent from the rhetoric of the cluster college. There was also a fundamental reconsideration of how important participation in an intimate academic community of a cluster college was to most students. In earlier attempts to create residential colleges, the small environment was always perceived as the central feature of the undergraduate experience, catering to the most conventional students. His racial and ethnic biases notwithstanding, Lawrence Lowell saw the house system as an instrument to provide a common experience for Harvard College's disparate student body.

But at Santa Cruz and most of the cluster college projects of the 1960s, the intimacy of the small college environment was aimed at students seeking an unconventional learning environment. Bearing out the Handlins' contention regarding the conditions in which such a project might succeed, the cluster college experience was offered as an alternative to what was correctly presumed to be the mainstream experience for most undergraduates; attendance in a large university with little faculty contact outside the classroom. John Hannah acknowledged that the small college experience was not for all, as many students preferred to operate in the big-league environment of the large university.[20]

Operationally, considerable variation characterized the cluster college projects, both in terms of the proportion of an institution's student body included, and how closely the cluster colleges and the formal curriculum were connected. The programs established at the public universities in Michigan were typical of cluster colleges established at large universities. These were residentially-based, curricularly focused units that included only a small portion of those institutions' 30,000-plus student bodies. In some instances, however, institutions were less interested in tying the curriculum to the cluster colleges. The State University of New York's campus at Stony Brook, for example, was organized around residential colleges with no formal tie to the curriculum: like Yale's residential colleges, they were conceived primarily as places where faculty and students could interact away from the classroom.[21]

Opinions on the optimal size of a cluster college also varied. Generally speaking, most institutions opted to establish cluster colleges that were somewhat larger than those envisioned by the earlier generation of residential college advocates. Commensurate with the expansion of the size of many institutions of higher education, the definition of "small college" grew progressively larger between 1930 and 1960. In the 1920s there was general consensus that an effective student community might range from 100 to 300 students, about the same size as contemporary Oxbridge residential colleges. James Blaisdell preferred colleges of 100 to 150 students, as did Edward Harkness and James Gamble Rogers at Yale; Kerr MacMillan guessed that 200 students was optimal, while the planners of Harvard's house system, for practical as well as educational reasons, pushed the number into the mid-200s. In the late 1940s, to accommodate returning veterans, colleges at Harvard, Yale, and Claremont expanded with the intention that the enrollment eventually would be reduced to prewar levels, but these rollbacks never occurred. By the late 1950s, Harvard's houses grew to incorporate over 400 students each. At Claremont in the 1950s, the more conventional interpretation of "small college" found increasing acceptance, as the four existing colleges ranged in enrollment from 400 to more than 1,000. In the 1960s, Theodore Newcomb estimated that 300 to 400 was the optimal size for an association of students "in which the groups were large enough to provide a range of selectivity based upon individual preferences for companionship, but not so large that most individuals would at least recognize one another."[22]

Within the milieu of cluster college experiments there was even more variability in the size of a small college. On the larger end of the spectrum of smallness were the cluster colleges of the University of California at San Diego, which numbered from 1,500 to 2,500 students, and the five residential colleges established at three Michigan universities—Michigan State, Wayne State, and Michigan—each of which enrolled 1,200 students.

Conversely, enrollment in Oakland University's three cluster colleges was limited to 350 students each, and the University of the Pacific's three cluster colleges comprised approximately 250 students.[23]

Optimism buoyed the movement. So did a sense that the success of the cluster college, like that of its spiritual progenitor, the Oxbridge residential college, was inevitable. As with earlier attempts to create such colleges, there was a generally accepted notion that small communities were inherently good and that proximity with faculty would provide for intellectual exchange in everyday life. Consistent with this outlook, little attention was paid to how to assess the educational effectiveness of the colleges. This point was raised in 1966 by Alexander Astin, who noted that the rationale for such projects relied strongly on ill-defined notions that students at large universities inherently felt alienated and depersonalized. Astin chided campus administrators for focusing too narrowly on the administrative and not on the conceptual questions raised by the cluster college movement. He also noted that there was a reluctance on the part of these people to engage in evaluative research, because such activities implicitly acknowledged the existence of doubt concerning the efficacy of the cluster college concept.[24]

The tendency for proponents to be long on optimism and short on detailed analysis was also noted by Lloyd Ring, who observed that, in the case of Santa Cruz, much of the literature concerning campus planning was vividly descriptive but lacked specification. The planning documents and early catalogs, for example, included liberal doses of such phrases as "the essence of Oxford" and references to each college being "its own intellectual center of gravity," but there was little detail on what these phrases and concepts meant in operational terms.[25]

In the period after World War II, California was the nation's fastest growing state. Its population increased from 7 million to 10 million between 1940 and 1950 and reached 15 million by 1960. Until the late 1950s the public higher education needs were met by the University of California system, a polytechnic college, and several state colleges. At that time, the University of California system consisted of two multiversity campuses at Berkeley (19,344 students) and Los Angeles (16,488 students), smaller undergraduate colleges at Santa Barbara (2,941 students) and Riverside (1,081 students), an agricultural school at Davis, and a health sciences campus in San Francisco.[26]

In anticipation of continued population expansion through the 1960s, the state legislature in 1957 authorized the creation of three new campuses for the University of California. When Kerr assumed the university presidency in 1958, he insisted that future institutions not become as large as the Berkeley and Los Angeles campuses. He was interested in exploring ways to keep the next generation of large campuses from bearing the same impersonal stamp as the existing campuses. One of the new campuses, which was to be located in the San Jose region, south of metropolitan San Francisco, was a promising setting for putting Kerr's ideas to work. The site chosen for the campus was near the resort town of Santa Cruz, a community that offered little potential for housing or absorbing a major university with a large student population. The demographic considerations meant providing housing for a much larger proportion of the student body than at other UC campuses (at the same time, UCLA and Berkeley each provided on-campus housing for about 4,000 students).

The University of California, Santa Cruz, was officially organized in 1961, with McHenry as chancellor. McHenry, who had been Kerr's assistant for academic planning at Berkeley, was charged with developing a plan for the campus that would make it "appear to stay small as it grew larger." McHenry responded by proposing the creation of a campus built around a federation of small, residential colleges, and he based his rationale on three primary considerations. Two of these were consistent with reasons put forward by proponents of residential colleges of the past. First, McHenry observed that undergraduates, particularly underclassmen, were often poorly taught by specialized faculty members. Second, he hoped that the plan might "alleviate the impersonality that often affects large, monolithic universities. The third consideration dealt with locating the campus in Santa Cruz. Because the Santa Cruz campus would need more extensive housing accommodations than other University of California campuses, regardless of its internal organization, McHenry urged that the collegiate plan be considered.[27]

In 1962 the Board of Regents approved a master plan for Santa Cruz that called for a residential college–based campus. This plan stipulated that developing a strong liberal arts–oriented undergraduate program was to be the faculty and administration's central mission during the first years of operation.[28] In the course of carrying out the regent's charge, McHenry revived many of the Oxbridge-inspired ideas of the first three decades of the twentieth century. Like James R. Angell, he also saw the residential college as an organizational module for orderly expansion as the university grew larger. Like Wilson and Lowell, McHenry hoped that the new organizational units would allow students to embrace both the intellectual and social aspects of their education. McHenry expected the residential college structure of Santa Cruz to help move the curriculum away from a permissive, free-elective system, and place greater emphasis on a core of basic subjects, to discourage early academic specialization, and to provide ample opportunity for independent study and honors work. Even the emphasis on sport, an important element of Aydelotte's notion of the "Oxford Stamp," was included, as McHenry stressed the importance of establishing an "extensive system of intramural athletics." Noting many of the trends regarding optimal size for residential colleges, McHenry and his staff determined that 600 students, with about 400 in residence, was the target size for Santa Cruz's colleges, adding that this figure was close to the size of colleges at more recently established English universities. Each college would also include fifty or so faculty fellows, drawn from a variety of disciplines, who would teach classes, maintain offices, and oversee the academic program of the colleges. All of the colleges included a house for a chief academic officer, who was called the provost, and several included accommodations for resident faculty as well.[29]

Santa Cruz's pioneer faculty and students took seriously the campus position as an experiment that might repattern the rest of higher education. They hoped that the new school could show how large universities might resist the compromises Kerr spelled out in his description of the multiversity. The student newspaper chose the name the *City on a Hill Press,* echoing the belief held by Boston Puritans of the seventeenth century that their model Christian commonwealth was the key to the spiritual redemption of the Old World.[30]

Beginning with the founding of Cowell College in 1965, one new college opened every year for the first eight years. Each college had an interdisciplinary academic emphasis that would serve as the genius loci for each college. Cowell emphasized the liberal arts; Stevenson College's (1966) theme, Self and Society, was based on modern social sciences; Crown's (1967) theme, Technology and Society, stressed the hard sciences; Merrill (1968) focused on Third World issues; Porter (1969) emphasized aesthetic philosophy and the fine arts; Kresge's (1970) theme was Man and his Environment; Oakes College (1971) stressed minority issues; and College VIII (1972) centered on environmental planning. On these bases the colleges developed their own core curriculum, which was expected to occupy about half of the course work during their first and second years. The plan also called for very large sections of introductory course work, thus freeing up faculty time for small upper-division courses, where tutorial methods might be employed.[31]

The physical landscape of the campus, though reflecting contemporary architectural thought in many ways, was well within the tradition established by James Gamble Rogers and Charles Coolidge in the 1920s. Santa Cruz's 1962 master plan called for the creation of college environments in language that might well have been used to describe Oxbridge colleges: "The individual colleges should be inward looking, with some aspect of a 'walled city' expressing a concept of self-contained unity."[32] In the interest of providing architectural diversity and of fostering distinct identities, the construction of the colleges was to be overseen by different architectural firms. The first five colleges (Cowell, Stevenson, Crown, Merrill, and Porter), although differing in execution and style, all opened inward onto adjoining courtyards. Adherence to the English pattern of enclosed, inward-looking colleges may have indeed been contrary to what was most appropriate in terms of design, given the topography: a student analysis of the design at Santa Cruz noted that the "architects and the planners were at the mercy of an ultimately alien model of the concept 'college,' which was not drawn from any American source, but explicitly from the medieval colleges of Britain."

Of the four original colleges, which were on the western side of the campus, Cowell commanded a view of Monterey Bay, but only from its public buildings, not from its residential courtyards. Stevenson, Crown, and Merrill colleges sacrificed their vistas to retain an inward-looking nature. Likewise, Porter College, located on the eastern side of UC Santa Cruz, was almost entirely enclosed. The informality of the stucco and tile-roofed California architecture of most of the colleges was described as a "humane way to democratize the privileges of an elitist education." In addition to the colleges, the campus included a core of facilities considered too expensive or impractical to duplicate among the colleges. These included science laboratories, central administration buildings, and a main library. Underscoring the centrality of the college to student social life, no union or activities center was planned for the campus.[33]

McHenry and Kerr were both concerned that the colleges fulfill their educational and social roles without being overrun by the conventional structure of the university, in which academic departments wielded considerable curricular authority and played a major role in resource allocation. The relation between academic departments and residential colleges had been a central feature of discussions in earlier attempts to create residential colleges. At Harvard and Yale, the academic departments remained paramount in matters of academic governance, a development that effectively kept the residential colleges and houses from becoming true centers of intellectual activity. At Claremont, on the other hand, the colleges maintained their own departments, often duplicating instruction and isolating disciplinary peers from one another. McHenry hoped that the Santa Cruz plan could be developed in such a way as to avoid the coordination problems between colleges that existed at Claremont. His head of academic planning, Byron Stookey, believed strongly that the college system itself would be undermined if academic departments controlled major academic functions, such as budgets, degree requirements, and hiring and promotion decisions.[34]

Stookey's concern over the power of academic departments was evidenced by the rather weak structure of disciplinary governance in early campus plans. As originally conceived, Santa Cruz faculty were organized into three broad divisions: humanities, social sciences, and natural sciences. The colleges and divisions were to bear jointly the costs of faculty appointments and to have an equal voice in hiring and tenure issues. This arrangement, however, proved too broad for the sensibilities of faculty, and in 1965 the Academic Senate authorized the creation of "boards of study," each representing a disciplinary area of study but without the sphere of control associated with a full-fledged department. When the idea of the boards was first discussed, McHenry advocated that they be small appointive bodies that served as boards of examiners, as at Oxford. This position, however, was not adopted. When the boards were enacted by the Academic Senate, all members of the discipline in question were appointed as ex officio members, rendering the boards much closer to academic departments in composition than planners originally intended.[35]

Although the impetus for developing Santa Cruz as a residential college–based campus represented a renascence for what were essentially conservative reform ideas, the experimental identity that Santa Cruz and other cluster college projects obtained also made them logical magnets for academic pioneering. Two of the most visible manifestations on unconventional practice at Santa Cruz were the use of nonstandard grading methods and the experimental curriculum developed at Kresge College. Shortly after the Academic Senate was organized at Santa Cruz, Cowell College faculty asked to replaced the conventional grading system with a pass/fail system, with letter grades in science courses available on student request. This system was ultimately adopted campuswide, but the performance evaluation was supplemented by a narrative evaluation by the instructor in all but the largest lecture classes.[36] Kresge College was based on an offshoot of humanistic psychology that sociologists Gerald Grant and David Riesman called a "communal expressive ideal." The official theme of Kresge was Man and his Environment, and the college sought to explore educational innovation through a human relations movement. College planners drew much of their inspiration from the ideas of psychologist Carl Rogers. Kresge's first provost, Robert Edgar, was a microbiologist who had become interested in humanistic psychology after Rogers conducted a series of workshops at Cal Tech, where Edgar was teaching. Edgar was interested in exploring ways to improve the quality of relationships between students and faculty, hoping to create what he called a "straight-talk community," emphasizing sensitivity training and organization of students around semifamilial "kin-groups."[37]

Throughout the 1960s, a spirit of optimism prevailed at Santa Cruz, fueled by the opening of new colleges and healthy growth in enrollment. By the early 1970s, however, this optimism had been replaced by feelings of demoralization and stagnation. The immediate impetus for this change was the flattening enrollment in the California state system of higher education, a trend that hit Santa Cruz especially hard. The selectivity of Santa Cruz's student body also slumped. In the mid-1960s, the Scholastic Aptitude Test scores of the student body were comparable to those of Princeton students. By 1975, they were closer to those of students at the State University of New York at Stony Brook, and Santa Cruz was in competition with UC Riverside for the dubious honor of being the system's most underenrolled site. The campus that had planned to equal Berkeley and Los Angeles in size peaked at one-third of its projected enrollment, prompting the Board of Regents to cancel plans for professional programs.[38]

The disproportionate drop in enrollment exacerbated the problems that had arisen as the collegial academic program developed. Experiments like the Narrative Evaluation System and Communal Structure at Kresge College were partly responsible for establishing a negative perception of Santa Cruz in the public eye, a view that was, according to David Riesman, abetted by Santa Cruz's lack of an engineering program or other technically oriented programs to offset the accusation of a "soft" curricular emphasis.[39] But experimentation was not the only variable in the changes that affected Santa Cruz after enthusiasm over the novelty of the the campus subsided. At the root of Santa Cruz's troubles was the residential college organization itself, which appeared to be unraveling. In its first decade of operation, the core curricula were largely abandoned, plans to develop tutorial instruction failed, and students increasingly rejected the notion of living within a tight-knit academic community and instead chose to live off campus.

A major source of difficulty for Santa Cruz was the idea of the college itself. The notion that the academic theme of the college would engender a genius loci was an operational failure. As Santa Cruz political scientist George von der Muhll observed, requiring each college to harbor members of every discipline on campus assured that faculty would be more or less attuned to the academic focus of the college, depending on how close their discipline lay to the college theme. Consequently, some faculty were deeply involved with the core curricula, while others occupied only peripheral roles. A second problem was that the core curricula system itself was not entirely popular either with faculty or students. Many students resisted the core curriculum, which they viewed as impinging on their ability to formulate a course of study. This resistance, coupled with faculty members' increasing lack of interest in teaching required courses, led to the rapid diminution of core courses in the colleges. Additionally, faculty, already pressured to fulfill research requirements for tenure, were overtaxed by the emphasis on interaction with undergraduates. Others faculty felt that it was difficult to obtain a sense of academic direction without graduate and professional schools.[40]

The experience of Cowell College was illustrative of this

process. In 1965, the core course at Cowell entitled "World Civilization" ran throughout students' freshman and sophomore years and encompassed one-third of the lower-division instructional program. Students, however, were unhappy with what they viewed as overprescription in their academic schedules, and they demanded more electives. The administration bowed to this pressure, and the second year of the core course was dropped in 1968; by 1971 the course consisted of a single quarter-long class. The other colleges had also truncated their core courses by the early 1970s.[41] Only the great books–oriented core course at Stevenson College continued throughout the freshman year; the core courses at all of the other colleges were shortened to one quarter (ten weeks).

The planned emphasis on tutorial and individualized instruction faltered along with the core courses. The idea that large lower-division sections would facilitate smaller upper-division tutorials and seminars failed to appreciate that the ratios were still too large for effective tutorials. Equally important, few faculty knew how to provide this kind of instruction.[42]

The cohesion of the colleges was further weakened because many students increasingly preferred to live off campus. In the early 1970s, Grant and Riesman found Santa Cruz undergraduates exhilarated by their academic environment. Over time, an increasing number of those students rejected the notion that residence in college was vital to the educational experience. Throughout the 1960s and 1970s, students increasingly preferred to live off campus. The percentage of the student body living on campus dropped from 81 percent to 66 percent in 1970. The reasons most students reported were connected to feeling too confined to the residential college community. In the mid-1970s, when only 50 percent of students lived on campus, many students viewed campus life as desirable for the first two years, allowing them to make social connections, but then preferred to live off campus. As Paul Woodring observed, many prospective freshmen had been socialized into functioning in large institutions by attending urban or suburban high schools larger than many denominational colleges.[43] In contrast, Oxford and Cambridge at the time of the conceptualization of the Oxbridge myth were populated largely by public school "old boys"—students who had been socialized into functioning in intensely communal environments from an early age.

In 1967, at the height of optimism about the cluster college movement, Paul Dressel speculated that the demands of specialization and departmentalization from both faculty and students might force modification of the collegial structure at Santa Cruz.[44] Within five years his prediction was borne out. In the wake of the academic difficulty experienced by the colleges, faculty and administrators increasingly turned to some form of departmentalism. Beginning in the mid-seventies, successive administrative reform efforts curtailed the curricular autonomy of the colleges and vested increased power in the boards of study, which did not grow into full-fledged academic departments, but which did replace the colleges as the primary organs of academic policy.

In late 1974, Santa Cruz's season of malaise, several faculty members put forward thoughts on reform, setting off a wave of discussion of possible reform efforts. Later, the Academic Senate's Budget and Academic Planning Committee presented a motion calling for the "reaggregation" of faculty into colleges to create critical masses of disciplinary colleagues. The motion received support from a number of faculty who felt that the curricular themes of the college had become unimportant. After initial support, however, aspects of reaggregation met considerable resistance from other faculty who were comfortable in their colleges, despite separation from disciplinary colleagues. In vain, the Budget and Academic Planning Committee insisted that colleges commit themselves to predefined academic clusters. These admonitions were unheeded, because the central administration did not stand behind the committee. Whatever reaggregation occurred was prompted more by the personal characteristics of individual faculty members and came to be described as "something resembling a fraternity rush."[45]

In November 1975, McHenry's successor, Chancellor Mark Christiensen, put forward his own reorganization plan: it sought to realign the colleges according to clusters of academic disciplines. Christiensen proposed abolishing the divisions of humanities and social sciences and relating their Boards of Studies to specific colleges. The natural sciences division would become a separate school. Faculty resistance to the proposal was strong, and the Academic Senate refused to consider the plan. The intensity of faculty opposition, coupled with the lack of administrative decisiveness during the reaggregation controversy, led to Christiensen's resignation as chancellor after only eighteen months in office.[46]

Ultimately, the equality of the matrices shifted in favor the Boards of Study. The colleges thus lost much of their power. A major reorganization took place under Chancellor Robert Sinsheimer, who took office in 1979, aimed at resolving the tension between the colleges and the boards of study, a situation described by Sinsheimer as a "state of dynamic immobility." The dual appointment system, which had made tenure and promotion a particularly clumsy and difficult process, was transferred completely to the Boards of Study. Most responsibility for curriculum planning was also removed from the colleges, and assigned to the Boards of Study. Most colleges continued to program introductory courses for freshmen only. Additionally, the explicit description of residential colleges as intellectual communities was superseded by passing references to the idea in the 1970–80 Proposed Academic Plan. Creating departments per se out of the Boards of Study was seen as a more effective way for Santa Cruz to deal with resource allocation and program quality.[47]

In the aftermath of reorganization, the colleges settled into their more limited educational roles. As George von der Muhll observed, Santa Cruz's eight colleges in the 1980s continued to "faithfully feed and house the majority of their students but no longer seek to reorient their minds." Some faculty continued to take an active part in the life of the college, but it was far smaller than that of their counterparts in the 1960s. The colleges did, however, acquire a renewed sense of purpose in the early 1980s by acquiring jurisdiction over many of the student affairs functions that had been assigned to other administrative departments. These included orienting new students and tending to students' nonacademic and personal needs. These functions were primarily assigned to professional staff.[48]

Throughout the 1980s the character of the student body at Santa Cruz drifted back toward its more conventional siblings in the University of California system. In the late 1980s, several of the sources of innovativeness also faded from view: Students were increasingly opting for letter grades in upper-level classes, while such majors as science, business, computer science, and communications were becoming more popular. Construction was begun on a student union. Rugby was even gaining popularity. Santa Cruz was not necessarily becoming a homogenized campus within a large state system, however. It still lacked representation by the kinds of students who fuel the conventional social life of college campuses, the "playboys and jocks" that Lawrence Lowell tried so hard to coax into the Harvard residential system.[49]

Even though the colleges have ceased to be centers of academic governance, the notion of collegial identity has remained important to many students. In 1986 the Student Union Assembly commissioned a task force to study Sinsheimer's policies with regard to the future role of the colleges in the academic life of the campus. The task force strongly advocated a return to collegial authority but recognized that this was unlikely. Expressions of concern over the role of the colleges in providing viable communities arose in response to efforts by a national Greek-letter fraternity to establish a chapter at Santa Cruz. In 1987, after Theta Chi fraternity took steps toward forming a chapter at Santa Cruz, campus opinion was mixed. There was significant resistance to the idea by students, and numerous letters sent to the university testified in opposition. This interest revealed that some members of the student body still cherished the alternative reputation attached to Santa Cruz. An organization called Students Against Greek Establishment (SAGE) was even organized to oppose fraternities. A task force appointed by Sinsheimer to study the question of fraternities at Santa Cruz took the controversy as an opportunity to reaffirm its commitment to the viability of the college system, if given favorable circumstances for development. The task force report noted that interest in fraternities and sororities was rooted in the same frustration that affected a large number of Santa Cruz students, a frustration that might be addressed by attempts to rekindle a spirit of community within the context of the colleges. This included recommending more extensive discussion of proposals for revitalizing the quality of the residential, social, and academic experiences of the colleges.[50]

Santa Cruz, like Harvard, had ambitious plans for its colleges, but when their relation to the university crystallized, they did not bring the life of the mind out of the classroom and into the student's home, although they provided congenial quarters that might not have existed otherwise. Like Puritan Boston, the latter-day City on a Hill did not live up to its original goal, but it developed merits of its own nonetheless. Santa Cruz of 1990 might have pleased James Gamble Rogers or Lawrence Lowell, but it would have disappointed James Rowland Angell or James Blaisdell. It is possible, however, that Santa Cruz may yet develop a workable college system based, if for no other reason than that, like Oxford and Cambridge, the campus is physically organized around enclosed clusters of buildings in which faculty teach and work, and in which students live. The colleges of Oxbridge, after all, went through a number of transformations of purpose and relationship to society before they emerged as the organs of a modern research university. For the present, however, Santa Cruz provided yet another example of how the pervasiveness of the Oxbridge residential college idea fueled a disappointing attempt at academic innovation.

Conclusion

In the early twentieth century, a group of American educators seized on the idea of using the organization of Oxbridge as a way to address perceived deficiencies in their own institutions of higher education. Specifically, reformers hoped to organize the undergraduate divisions of research universities around small academic communities modeled after the Oxbridge residential college, to solve to a variety of institutional ills connected to growth in size and the increasing importance of research and graduate education. These issues retained currency throughout the century. Not surprisingly, residential college plans continued to be offered in response.

In the 1890s, Harvard faculty and alumni saw the residential college as a way to provide a coherent social life for an increasingly diverse and nonresidential undergraduate student body. A decade later, Woodrow Wilson saw the college as a way to arrest the anti-intellectual tendencies of Princeton's students. In the 1920s, James Blaisdell of Pomona College hoped that creating a federation of small colleges would prevent the emergence of a large and impersonal institution and would generate the sense of intellectual colloquy between students and faculty he associated with Oxford colleges. Conversely, in the 1960s, an era in which large multiversities increasingly dominated systems of higher education, Clark Kerr and Dean McHenry revived the residential college idea in an attempt to demonstrate that a very large university did not necessarily need to be an impersonal one.

None of these efforts lived up to the expectations of their framers, save for those whose goals were vague or simplistic in the first place, such as Edward Harkness. But with the exception of the planners of the University of California, Santa Cruz, the authors of even the most detailed and well-developed plans often based their ideas on only limited exposure to the workings of Oxford and Cambridge, relying on conventional and often romanticized notions of life and work in the venerable English universities. While Clark Kerr and Dean McHenry were certainly better informed about the inner workings of Oxford and Cambridge, they nevertheless set educational goals for Santa Cruz that were inadequately defined and supported.[1] All but the most skeptical observers continued to believe that close faculty and student contact as well as a strong sense of identity would somehow arise from the intimate and congenial surroundings of a collegelike setting. Function, in this instance, was seen as following form.

The idea of importing the Oxbridge-style residential college to America took form in an era marked by often exaggerated claims of a common bond of sympathy with England. It is therefore not difficult to see why some Americans would underestimate the difficulty of adapting one "Anglo-Saxon" societal institution into another setting that appeared to fall well within the bounds of a common culture. But important differences existed not only within the organizational patterns of English and American university life but also between English and American educational systems and between English and American society at large. Those who favored Anglicizing the American university, however, were not attuned to significant differences; they were far more interested in the commonalities.

Even after the intense Anglophilia of the early twentieth century had dissipated, the notion of the life of the small college within a large university continued to have power, especially as many universities became as large and complex as small cities. The residue of earlier and only partially successful attempts did not discourage the next generation of residential college advocates. If anything, the presence of Harvard's houses, Yale's colleges, and many more buildings on college campuses across America that mimicked the appearance of Oxford and Cambridge without attempting to copy their organizational pattern provided visual inspiration to the educators who kept the notion of the residential college in circulation.

Some of the blame for the disappointing results of these projects may be assigned to the tendency of residential college proponents to pay close attention to the organizational structure of Oxford and Cambridge without examining the social contexts within which they operated. As a result, some important features of the residential college pattern were misinterpreted. Residential college proponents underplayed the importance of the relationship between the English public school and the university. The public schools provided the colleges with students who were academically prepared to begin specialized scholarship. Further, the public school "old boys," who made up a considerable proportion of the Oxbridge student body, were already socialized into living in an intensely communal environment and had undergone a social apprenticeship prior to entering Oxford or Cambridge. By the time the English student arrived at his college, he possessed many of the social and intellectual attributes that Americans associated with the undergraduate experience. Relatedly, the English notion of close contact between undergraduate and teacher was, once again, based on their common interest in specialized scholarship.

Planners expressed great faith in the residential college's ability to unite students and faculty in a sense of academic community, but faith alone could not reconcile the demands of scholarly life with the roles that faculty members were expected to play as collegial community members. To his credit, Woodrow Wilson understood that his preceptors were being asked to relate to students in a way that might not suit research-oriented faculty, and he therefore attempted to lure experienced secondary school teachers to Princeton. He turned to journeyman scholars only as a last resort. The resistance of the academic departments of Harvard and Yale were strong enough to keep the role of the houses and residential colleges to a minimum. The tutors—the faculty members who had significant contact with residential college students—were most often graduate students themselves, or junior faculty whose involvement with students might come at the expense of activities needed for promotion or tenure. At Santa Cruz, where planners laid elaborate plans to head off divided loyalties between college and discipline, faculty were still answerable to University of California standards for promotion and tenure and were often worn down by serving both career and college. Claremont was the most successful in maintaining the integrity of the college, but the independent nature of the colleges made faculty feel isolated from disciplinary peers.

The continued interest in pursuing residential college projects and the consistent failure of these projects to create small, intimate communities of scholars and students also illustrates a more general point about academic innovation. Tradition and perceived notions about other institutions and educational systems may be just as powerful as reasoned inquiry and careful analysis in the development of academic plans. In most instances, the ideas that animated residential college proponents were based on minimal understanding of the workings of Oxford and Cambridge, and on even less understanding of the relation of these institutions to their broader social contexts. As Woodrow Wilson's comments to his wife illustrated, he was infatuated with Oxford before deciding to imitate its structure.

Likewise, James Blaisdell was only secondarily acquainted with the workings of Oxford before deciding that Pomona College ought to be based on an Oxford-like system of residential colleges. On balance, the ideas of these men were far more widely regarded than those of skeptics like Leon Richardson, or somewhat reluctant proponents, like James Rowland Angell.

It is perhaps too easy to criticize plans that ultimately failed; few people, after all, would willingly commit themselves to any undertaking if they knew that it was destined not to succeed. Some credit is certainly due the residential college proponents for their efforts; most were genuinely motivated by a desire to increase the quality of students' experience at times when undergraduate education appeared to be losing ground to graduate education and research. Although renewed attempts to establish residential colleges are unlikely in the near future (unless Santa Cruz's colleges unexpectedly gain new life), it is likely that some educators will continue to attempt to make the large university a more humane and hospitable environment. Perhaps putting to rest a century-old fixation with re-creating Oxford in America would allow educators the freedom to explore more original—and potentially more successful—ways to broaden the experience of undergraduates beyond the classroom.

Afterword

Since 1980 there have been no serious attempts to expand upon or revive the idea of Oxbridge-style residential colleges at the institutions cited in this study.

The Claremont Colleges have continued to operate as a cluster of largely self-contained American-style liberal arts colleges with generally complementary curricular offerings. Claremont Men's College became coeducational in 1976 and was renamed Claremont McKenna College, in honor of one of its trustees. With the exception of Pomona College, enrollments have continued to rise. Claremont McKenna College now enrolls more than 950 students; Pitzer, 750; Harvey Mudd, 645; and Scripps, over 600. No new colleges have been added or are under consideration.

The University of California, Santa Cruz, still consists of eight residential colleges, each professing a curricular theme. Seven of the eight colleges offer only one quarter-length course dedicated to the college theme, but Stevenson College still offers a one-year great books course that includes works drawn from nonwestern cultural traditions. The resident student body in all of the colleges is still predominantly freshmen and sophomores.

The Harvard houses and Yale colleges continue to operate as congenial residential quarters that provide a locus of social activity for undergraduate students, as well as some contact with professors. Selection procedures have recently been altered at both institutions. Harvard now permits groups of up to sixteen freshmen to apply to houses as a group, a practice somewhat suggestive of Princeton's "hat lines" of the pre–World War I era. Yale now assigns students to a college prior to the freshman year. Students live in the old campus dormitories during their freshman year but take their meals in the colleges.

Notes

Introduction

1. Like many terms in use in higher education—"chancellor," "college," and "university"—"residential college" is inexact in its definition. The designation may be applied to any institution of higher learning that houses at least part of its student body. For the sake of clarity, the term residential college will be used here to refer only to residential subunits at institutions that attempt to integrate the intellectual and social lives of students and faculty in the perceived fashion of the universities of Oxford and Cambridge, collectively referred to as "Oxbridge."

2. See Bragdon, *Woodrow Wilson: The Academic Years;* Craig, *Woodrow Wilson at Princeton;* Storr, *Harper's University: The Beginnings: A History of the University of Chicago;* Bergin, *Yale's Residential Colleges;* Jencks and Riesman, "Patterns of Residential Education." Also see Bernard, *Unfinished Dream;* Clary, *Claremont Colleges;* Lyon, *History of Pomona College.*

3. Gaff, "Cluster College Concept," 16–17, 9.

4. See McHenry, "Academic Organizational Matrix at Santa Cruz"; Von der Muhll, "University of California at Santa Cruz"; D. Davis, "Cluster College Revisited."

5. Harvard University Committee on the Objectives of a General Education in a Free Society, *General Education in a Free Society,* 7.

6. Horn et al., "Facilities and Learning," 155.

7. Veysey, *Emergence of the American University,* 21–56, 174–77.

8. Veysey, *Emergence of the American University,* 294–95.

9. Wenley, "Reckless Tenants," 32.

10. Handlin and Handlin, *American College and American Culture,* 85.

11. See W. Wilson, "Report on the Social Co-ordination of the University," *Princeton Alumni Weekly,* 12 June 1907, quoted in Slosson, *Great American Universities,* 79–80; Lowell, *At War with Academic Tradition;* and Jones, *Comprehensive Examinations in American Colleges.*

12. Thelin, *Higher Education and Its Useful Past,* 45.

13. Hamlin, "Educational Influence of Collegiate Architecture," 323.

14. See Lowe, "Anglo-Americanism in the Planning of Universities"; and Turner, *Campus*, 215-48.

15. See Engel, *From Clergyman to Don*, 5-22; Garland, *Cambridge Before Darwin*, 13-16; "Essays on a Professional Education by R. L. Edgeworth," 45-46; A. Smith, *Inquiry into the Nature and Causes of the Wealth of Nations;* "The Irish and English Universities," *Dublin Review* 1 (May 1836): 89-90; "Traité de Mechanique Céleste par P.S. La Place," 283-84; and Hamilton, "Universities of England—Oxford."

16. Newman, *Idea of a University*, 129-30.

17. B. Clark, *Higher Education System*, 82.

18. Shils, *Tradition*, 195. Shils acknowledged that his dichotomy between a noumenal and perceived past was inspired by Henri-Irénée Marrou, who applied Kant's terms of phenomena and noumena metaphorically to history. See Marrou, *Meaning of History*, 42-52.

I
The Paradox of the English Residential College

1. Samuel Eliot Morison, "An American Professor's Recollections on Oxford," *The Spectator*, 14 November, 1925, 811-66, quoted in Commager, *Britain Through American Eyes*, 696.

2. See principally Alexander, *Growth of English Education;* Brooke and Highfield, *Oxford and Cambridge;* Cobban, *Medieval English Universities;* Curtis, *Oxford and Cambridge in Transition;* Engel, *From Clergyman to Don;* Garland, *Cambridge Before Darwin;* Kearney, *Scholars and Gentlemen;* Lawson and Silver, *Social History of Education in England;* Mallet, *History of the University of Oxford;* Rothblatt, *Revolution of the Dons;* Wood, *Reformation and English Education.*

3. Cobban, *Medieval English Universities*, 161-64, 353-54; Lawson and Silver, *Social History of Education in England*, 31.

4. Cobban, *Medieval English Universities*, 153-54; Emden, *Oxford Hall in Medieval Times*, 7-59; Lawson and Silver, *Social History of Education in England*, 25. Cobban estimates the average number of residents per hall in fifteenth-century Oxford at about sixteen. At Cambridge the hostels were far less numerous but housed considerably more students. The hostels for legists averaged between eighty and one hundred, while those for artists (students in arts) houses twenty to forty each.

5. Lawson and Silver, *Social History of Education in England*, 29-30; Hamilton, "Universities of England—Oxford," 418-19; Cobban, *Medieval*

English Universities, 151–52. At Oxford, only six colleges existed before 1400, and only three more were added by 1450. At Cambridge, eight colleges existed before 1400, and five more were added by 1500. In contrast, the average number of halls at Oxford in the fifteenth century has been estimated by Alan Cobban at between sixty and seventy. The hostels at Cambridge in the same period were only one-fourth as numerous but were larger in size.

6. Cobban, *Medieval English Universities,* 302, 125; Lawson and Silver, *Social History of Education in England,* 29–30. Cobban notes that Oxford and Cambridge recruited from the lesser gentry, from wealthier peasant and yeomanry classes; from the families of village officials and from manorial society in rural areas, and from merchant and artisan families in towns.

7. Engel, *From Clergyman to Don,* 3; Hamilton, "Universities of England—Oxford," 395; Lawson and Silver, *Social History of Education in England,* 52.

8. Alexander, *Growth of English Education,* 157; Curtis, *Oxford and Cambridge in Transition,* 45–53, 71–72; Lawson and Silver, *Social History of Education in England,* 126–27, 129–30.

9. Kearney, *Scholars and Gentlemen,* 22–28; Wood, *Reformation and English Education,* 81–82; Lawson and Silver, *Social History of Education in England,* 126, 128–29.

10. Cobban, *Medieval English Universities,* 158.

11. Lawson and Silver, *Social History of Education in England,* 131; Hamilton, "Universities of England—Oxford," 412.

12. Curtis, *Oxford and Cambridge in Transition,* 272–73; Lawson and Silver, *Social History of Education in England,* 177.

13. Gibbon quoted in Thwing, *A History of Higher Education in America,* 126–27; A. Smith, *Inquiry into the Nature and Causes of the Wealth of Nations,* 250–51; Engel, *From Clergyman to Don,* 16–22; "Essays on a Professional Education by R. L. Edgeworth," 45–46.

14. Garland, *Cambridge Before Darwin,* 48–50; Buchloh and Rix, *American Colony of Göttingen,* 13–14; Hodgskin, *Travels in the North of Germany,* 273–74.

15. Copleston, *Reply to the Calumnies Against Oxford,* 111–12; Mallet, *History of the University of Oxford,* 183–84.

16. Copleston, *Reply to the Calumnies Against Oxford,* 182–83; Hamilton, "Universities of England—Oxford," 394; Mallet, *History of the University of Oxford,* 290–92.

17. Engel, *From Clergyman to Don,* 17–28.

18. Mallet, *History of the University of Oxford*, 168; Brooke and Highfield, *Oxford and Cambridge*, 274; Garland, *Cambridge Before Darwin*, 48–50, 127–292.

19. Engel, *From Clergyman to Don*, 18.

20. Engel, *From Clergyman to Don*, 18; Bill and Mason, *Christ Church and Reform*, 2–3, 25–26; Hamilton, "Universities of England—Oxford," 395.

21. Engel, *From Clergyman to Don*, 3.

22. Brooke and Highfield, *Oxford and Cambridge*, 273, 298;Engel, *From Clergyman to Don*, 156–201.

23. Rothblatt, *Revolution of the Dons*, 238–39.

24. Rothblatt, " 'Standing Antagonisms,' " 48; Honey, *Tom Brown's Universe*, 138–39; Rothblatt, *Revolution of the Dons*, 50.

25. Mangan, *Athleticism in the Victorian and Edwardian Public School*, 12–27.

26. Rothblatt, *Revolution of the Dons*, 193.

27. Symmonds, *Oxford and Empire*, 186–89.

28. Honey, *Tom Brown's Universe*, 153.

29. Sanderson, *Universities in the Nineteenth Century*, 3.

30. Parkin, *Rhodes Scholarships*, 213–14. University College, Oxford, traditionally listed its founding date as 872, and its founder as Alfred the Great. This claim is mentioned in one fourteenth-century chronicle but has no apparent corroboration. Cobban, *Medieval English Universities*, 20.

31. Brooke and Highfield, *Oxford and Cambridge*, 295–96.

32. K. Clark, *Gothic Revival*, 301.

33. Norwich, *Great Architecture of the World*, 212.

34. Ruskin, "Inaugural Address, Oriel College, 1870," as quoted in Aydelotte, *American Rhodes Scholars*, 3.

35. Newman, *Idea of a University*, 10.

36. Newman, *Idea of a University*, 130–31. The rest of this frequently cited passage is equally revealing about Newman's notions of the value of residential education: "Thus it is that, independent of direct instruction on the part of Superiors, there is a sort of self-education in the academic institutions of Protestant England; a characteristic tone of thought, a recognized standard of judgement is found in them, which, as developed in the individual who is submitted to it, becomes a twofold source of strength to him, both from the distinct stamp it impresses in his mind, and from the bond of union it creates between him and others—effects which are shared by the authorities of the place, for they themselves have been educated in it, and at all times are exposed to the influence of its ethical atmosphere. Here then is a real teaching, whatever be its standards and principles, true or false; and it at least tends toward cultivation of the

intellect; it at least recognizes that knowledge is something more than a sort of passive reception of scraps and details; it is something, and it does a something, which never will issue from the most strenuous efforts of a set of teachers, with no mutual sympathies and no intercommunion, of a set of examiners with no opinions which they dare profess, and with no common principles, who are teaching or questioning a set of youths who do not know them, and do not know each other, on a large number of subjects, different in kind, and connected by no wide philosophy, three times a week, or once in three years, in chill lecture-rooms, or on a pompous anniversary."

37. Arnold, *Culture and Anarchy;* Rothblatt, *Revolution of the Dons,* 124-29.
38. Brooke and Highfield, *Oxford and Cambridge,* 295-97. See also Attwater, *Pembroke College;* Robertson, *All Souls College;* Fowler, *History of Corpus Christi College;* H. Wilson, *Magdalen College.*
39. H. Davis, *History of Balliol College,* 173-74.
40. Peile, *Christ's College;* Rothblatt, *Revolution of the Dons,* 156, 211.
41. See Rothblatt, *Revolution of the Dons;* Engel, *From Clergyman to Don.*
42. Proctor, *English University Novel,* 1-2.
43. Proctor, *English University Novel,* 150-56.
44. Harold Hartley, "Benjamin Jowett: An Epilogue," in H. Davis, *History of Balliol College,* 200; Symmonds, *Oxford and Empire,* 3.
45. H. Davis, *History of Balliol College,* 3-17.
46. H. Davis, *History of Balliol College,* 180-209.
47. H. Davis, *History of Balliol College,* 189-200; Scott, *A. D. Lindsay,* 108.
48. Symmonds, *Oxford and Empire,* 186-89; Haines, "Second Reform of Cambridge and Oxford," 115.
49. H. Davis, *History of Balliol College,* 100, 40, 180.
50. Mackail, *James Leigh Strachan-Davidson,* 54-56, 64-65.
51. Mackail, *James Leigh Strachan-Davidson,* 64-65, 124; Scott, *A. D. Lindsay,* 45, 57, 106, 110.

2

The Whole Man and the Gentleman Scholar

1. See Veysey, *Emergence of the American University;* Brubacher and Rudy, *Higher Education in Transition,* 174-97.
2. Veysey, *Emergence of the American University,* 194-212; Rudolph, *Curriculum: A History of the American Undergraduate Course of Study,* 174. See also Geiger, *To Advance Knowledge,* 115-23.
3. W. Wilson, "Spirit of Learning," 7, 9-10.

4. Veysey, *Emergence of the American University*, 212–13.

5. Brubacher and Rudy, *Higher Education in Transition*, 111–13; Lowell, "Inaugural Address," 211.

6. Cowley, "Influences upon American Higher Education," 184; Turner, *Campus*, 216; Lowell, "Inaugural Address," 211–12;Corbin, *Which College for the Boy?* 114.

7. W. Wilson, "Spirit of Learning," 7; Slosson, *Great American Universities*, 506.

8. Corbin, *Which College for the Boy?* 100–106, 198–99; Wertenbaker, *Princeton*, 281–83, 322–23.

9. Brubacher and Rudy, *Higher Education in Transition*, 131–36.

10. Lowell, "Inaugural Address," 212. Theodore Rader has argued that in the late nineteenth century the displacement of older geographic communities prompted Americans to establish new forms of community. Sport clubs began to assume the traditional function of church, state, and geographic community, and some ended up with large followings. For a general discussion of the role of sports in college during the Progressive Era, see Noverr and Ziewacz, *Games They Played.*

11. W. Wilson, "Spirit of Learning," 3; Cowley, "Influences upon American Higher Education," 183.

12. Slosson, *Great American Universities*, 12–13; Veysey, *Emergence of the American University*, 182: "It might seem plain enough, at least, that the advocates of liberal culture constituted a minority in American academic circles. But the militant insistence of the humanists partly compensated for their paucity of numbers. So vocal were they that, especially toward the end of the period, they wrote considerably more about the problems of higher education than did the advocates of research. If they were under-representative of most of the larger universities, still they commanded the official platforms of some of the more 'up-to-date' small colleges. The bravado of their rhetoric was such that their failure to win real power seems almost surprising in retrospect."

13. Thwing, *Universities of the World*, 3.

14. Hawes, *Twenty Years Among the Twenty Year Olds*, 56; Cowley, "History of College Residential Housing I," 708; Lowell, "Higher Education and Its Present Task."

15. Gilman, *University Problems in the United States*, 304–5.

16. Mirroring the efforts of conservative American educators to invoke an idealized picture of Oxford, American Progressives held up the former English colonies of Australia and particularly New Zealand as socialist

exemplars as they pressed for social reform. See Coleman, *Progressivism and the World of Reform.*

17. Kaestle, *Pillars of the Republic,* 177.
18. Commager, *Britain Through American Eyes,* xx–xxi; Shils, *Tradition,* 208.
19. Commager, *Britain Through American Eyes,* xxi–xxii.
20. Commager, *Britain Through American Eyes,* 214; Thwing, *Universities of the World,* 21.
21. Burton, "Theodore Roosevelt and the 'Special Relationship' with Britain." Roosevelt received an honorary degree from Oxford in 1910, and his son Kermit served as a volunteer in the British Air Corps during World War I. Sir George Clark, as quoted in Burton, "Theodore Roosevelt and the 'Special Relationship' with Britain," 535.
22. Commager, *Britain Through American Eyes,* xxxvii.
23. Cram, *Significance of Gothic Art,* 2.
24. Cram, *Ministry of Art,* 46.
25. Cram, *Ministry of Art,* 46–47.
26. Turner, *Campus,* 227–33 (Woodrow Wilson to Edith Wilson, 26 July 1899, quoted on 227; West quoted on 233; W. Wilson quoted on 227).
27. Canby, *Alma Mater,* 79.
28. Bristed, *Five Years in an English University,* vi–vii.
29. Hill, *Harvard College by an Oxonian,* 316, 327.
30. Commager, *Britain Through American Eyes,* 568–69; Corbin, *American at Oxford,* 77.
31. Corbin, *American at Oxford,* vi, 177.
32. Corbin, *American at Oxford,* 131.
33. Corbin derived the term "hall" not from the standard parlance of a hall as any academic building, but from the medieval *aulau,* the term for a self-directed student residence of the medieval university (*American at Oxford,* 302).
34. Corbin, *American at Oxford,* 322, vi–vii.
35. Hill, *Harvard College by an Oxonian,* 316.
36. Aydelotte, *American Rhodes Scholars,* 15; Thwing, *American and German University,* 71–73.
37. Aydelotte, *American Rhodes Scholars,* 18; Symmonds, *Oxford and Empire,* 164–65.
38. Harris, "Oxford University and the Rhodes Scholarships," 268; *Boston Evening Transcript* quoted in "American at Oxford," 320–21.
39. Harris, "Oxford University and the Rhodes Scholarships," 278.
40. Aydelotte, *American Rhodes Scholars,* 133. In 1992, Bill Clinton became

the first Rhodes Scholar to be elected to the U.S. presidency. This event should have signaled the culmination of Cecil Rhodes's efforts to foster pro-English sentiment among American political elites. But Clinton's election campaign call for international intervention in Northern Ireland, and his decision to allow banned Sinn Fein leader Gerry Adams to visit the United States, marked the first time a U.S. presidential candidate proposed altering the special relationship between Britain and the United States.

41. In addition to Aydelotte, Lyon, Buchanan, and Barr, this group included G. K. Chalmers (Kenyon College); V. M. Hancher (Iowa State University); C. F. Gates (University of Denver); Frederick L. Hovde (Purdue University); H. G. Hudson (Illinois College); John O. Mosely (University of Nevada at Reno); John W. Nason (Swarthmore); J. J. Tigert (University of Florida); and Alan Valentine (University of Rochester) (Aydelotte, *American Rhodes Scholars*, 134–208).

42. Aydelotte, *Oxford Stamp*, 5–6.

43. Aydelotte, *Oxford Stamp*, 5–6.

44. Aydelotte, *Oxford Stamp*, 8.

45. Aydelotte, *Oxford Stamp*, 58.

46. Coffin, "Paradox of Oxford," 170–73.

47. Beerbohm, *Zuleika Dobson*, 87. Beerbohm lampooned the Rhodes Scholars in the character of of the Abimalech B. Oover, an ever-orating Yale-educated anabaptist from Pittsburg [*sic*], who was "sorely tried by the quaint old English custom of not making public speeches after private dinners." *Sinister Street;* Scott, *A. D. Lindsay*, 109–10.

48. Veysey, *Emergence of the American University*, 252. See Lowell, "Inaugural Address," 211–12; W. Wilson, "What Is a College For?" 574.

3
Early Attempts: Harvard, Chicago, and Princeton

1. Slosson, *Great American Universities*, 22, 41, 109.

2. Slosson, *Great American Universities*, 25, 33.

3. Thayer, "Germanization, Oxfordization and Critics," 283–84.

4. Slosson, *Great American Universities*, 18.

5. Riesman, "Education at Harvard," 25; Jencks and Riesman, "Patterns of Residential Education," 736–77.

6. Hawes, *Twenty Years Among the Twenty Year Olds*, 134–41; Corbin, *Which College for the Boy?* 56–57; Lowell, "Dormitories and College Life," 527.

7. Bolles, "Administrative Problem," 6–7.

8. *Harvard Graduate's Magazine,* June 1904, 704; Twombly, "College Hall System," 585–88.

9. Pratt, "Undergraduate Plan," 592.

10. Adams, "Ideal College Organization," 202.

11. Beale, "Reorganization of the University," 33.

12. Lowell, *At War with Academic Tradition,* 28–29.

13. Hart, "The Critic's, and the Real Harvard."

14. Thayer, "Germanization, Oxfordization and Critics," 284.

15. Charles W. Eliot, quoted in Yeomans, *Abbott Lawrence Lowell,* 167–68.

16. Slosson, *Great American Universities,* 41.

17. Brubacher and Rudy, *Higher Education in Transition,* 336.

18. Vincent quoted in Block, *Uses of Gothic,* 62; Slosson, *Great American Universities,* 41.

19. Brubacher and Rudy, *Higher Education in Transition,* 254.

20. Thompson, "House System," 390–92.

21. Thompson, "House System," 387–88.

22. Thompson, "House System," 387.

23. Thompson, "House System," 387.

24. Storr, *Harper's University,* 322.

25. Storr, *Harper's University,* 322.

26. Storr, *Harper's University,* 320–27.

27. Slosson, *Great American Universities,* 42.

28. W. Wilson, "Report on the Social Co-ordination of the University," *Princeton Alumni Weekly,* 12 June 1907, quoted in Slosson, *Great American Universities,* 79–80.

29. By the time that Woodrow Wilson became president in 1902, Princeton's enrollment exceeded 1,200 undergraduate and 100 graduate students (Slosson, *Great American Universities,* 109).

30. Wertenbaker, *Princeton,* 342.

31. Leslie, *Gentlemen and Scholars,* 124–25.

32. Craig, *Woodrow Wilson at Princeton,* 67–68.

33. Wertenbaker, *Princeton,* 281–83, 322–23.

34. Wertenbaker, *Princeton,* 31, 358.

35. Slosson, *Great American Universities,* 103; Corbin, *Which College for the Boy?* 30.

36. Slosson, *Great American Universities,* 101–02; Bragdon, *Woodrow Wilson: The Academic Years,* 318.

37. Baker, *Woodrow Wilson: Life and Letters,* 75; Veysey, "Academic Mind of Woodrow Wilson," 630, 626, 622.

38. Craig, *Woodrow Wilson at Princeton*, 7; Spaeth quoted in Myers, *Woodrow Wilson: Some Princeton Memories*, 83.

39. Baker, *Woodrow Wilson: Life and Letters*, 215, 80.

40. Craig, *Woodrow Wilson at Princeton*, 74–80; Link, *Wilson: The Road to the White House*, 41–42; Leslie, *Gentlemen and Scholars*, 120–24, 150–52.

41. Leitch, *Princeton Companion*, 374.

42. W. Wilson, "Address before the Undergraduate Press Club, Princeton, 15 April 1905," as quoted in Link, *Wilson: The Road to the White House*, 41.

43. Bragdon, *Woodrow Wilson: The Academic Years*, 365–66.

44. Bragdon, *Woodrow Wilson: The Academic Years*, 319.

45. Wilson's notes from the "Supplementary Report to the Trustees," as quoted in Baker, *Woodrow Wilson: Life and Letters*, 220; Craig, *Woodrow Wilson at Princeton*, 119.

46. Bragdon, *Woodrow Wilson: The Academic Years*, 319; Link, *Wilson: The Road to the White House*, 56.

47. Craig, *Woodrow Wilson at Princeton*, 102.

48. Veysey, *Emergence of the American University*, 244; Turner, *Campus*, 230, 233.

49. Bragdon, *Woodrow Wilson: The Academic Years*, 334.

50. Yeomans, *Abbott Lawrence Lowell*, 356.

51. Lowell "Self-Education in Harvard College," 70; Hawes, *Twenty Years Among the Twenty Year Olds*, 156; Corbin, *Which College for the Boy?* 30–32.

52. Flexner, *American College*, 208; Leitch, *Princeton Companion*, 374–75.

53. Slosson, *Great American Universities*, 421.

54. Flexner, *American College*, 231.

4
The Harkness Bequests: Harvard Houses and Yale Colleges

1. *Yale Record*, 12 February 1929, quoted in Pierson, *Yale: The University College*, 208.

2. Geiger, *To Advance Knowledge*, 116–17.

3. Pierson, *Yale: The University College*, 65, 669–70; Synnott, *Half-Opened Door*, 14, 96. In the early 1920s, Harvard capped undergraduate enrollment at 1,000, and Yale College limited its student body to 850. Wechsler, *Qualified Student*, 3–4, 238, 245.

4. Yale College did not become coeducational until 1968. Radcliffe College, Harvard's undergraduate women's institution, remained largely separate from Harvard College until the 1950s. Yeomans, *Abbott Lawrence Lowell*,

209; Feldman, *Recruiting an Elite,* 7; Lipset, "Political Controversies at Harvard," 144–50, 179.

5. Wechsler, "An Academic Gresham's Law," 575–76, 580; Lipset, "Political Controversies at Harvard," 143.

6. Synnott, *Half-Opened Door,* 16–17, 123–59.

7. Leacock, *My Discovery of England,* 74.

8. See Richardson, *Study of the Liberal College.*

9. Richardson, *Study of the Liberal College,* 111, 159–61, 84.

10. Yeomans, *Abbott Lawrence Lowell,* 144.

11. Lowell, "Self-Education in Harvard College," 72, 66.

12. Veysey, *Emergence of the American University,* 250.

13. Morison, *Three Centuries of Harvard,* 446.

14. Yeomans, *Abbott Lawrence Lowell,* 144–46.

15. Lowell, "General Examinations and Tutors in Harvard College," 66.

16. Jones, *Comprehensive Examinations in American Colleges,* 251.

17. Lowell, "General Examinations and Tutors in Harvard College," 76.

18. Harvard University Committee on the Objectives of a General Education in a Free Society, *General Education in a Free Society,* 191.

19. Perkins, "Impersonal Oxford," 245–47.

20. Hindmarsh, "Harvard Educational Plan," 172.

21. Morison, *Three Centuries of Harvard,* 445–46, 462; Yeomans, *Abbott Lawrence Lowell,* 172–73.

22. Brown, *Dean Briggs,* 154; Turner, *Campus,* 244.

23. Pierson, *Yale: The University College,* 446–47, 211, 210.

24. Slosson, *Great American Universities,* 66–72.

25. Turner, *Campus,* 240; Canby, *Alma Mater,* 53.

26. Morison, *Three Centuries of Harvard,* 462.

27. MacMillan, "Ideals for an Effective College," 212–13.

28. Pierson, *Yale: The University College,* 213f.

29. Kelley, *Yale, A History,* 374; Pierson, *Yale: The University College,* 249–50ff.

30. Pierson, *Yale: The University College,* 16–17; Polkinghorne, *Methodology for the Human Sciences,* 192; Angell, "College Plan," in *American Education,* 260–61.

31. Angell, "College Plan," 267.

32. Pierson, *Yale: The University College,* 216.

33. Kelley, *Yale, A History,* 374.

34. Pierson, *Yale: The University College,* 220.

35. Pierson, *Yale: The University College,* 238–39.

36. Pierson, *Yale: The University College,* 238–39. See also Abbot Lawrence

Lowell, "The Division of Undergraduates into Residential Colleges (or Houses), April 19, 1907," in Lowell, *At War with Academic Tradition*.

37. Pierson, *Yale: The University College*, 239–40.
38. Morison, *Three Centuries of Harvard*, 476–77.
39. Pierson, *Yale: The University College*, 242.
40. Synnott, *Half-Opened Door*, 137; Yeomans, *Abbott Lawrence Lowell*, 191.
41. Pierson, *Yale: The University College*, 243–52.
42. Turner, *Campus*, 241; Morison, *Three Centuries of Harvard*, 477–78; Synnott, *Half-Opened Door*, 111–13; Yeomans, *Abbott Lawrence Lowell*, 224.
43. Bergin, *Yale's Residential Colleges*, 126–49; Turner, *Campus*, 241.
44. Pierson, *Yale: The University College*, 410; Turner, *Campus*, 244; Jencks and Riesman, "Patterns of Residential Education," 732.
45. Lowell, "Self-Education in Harvard College," 72; Angell, "College Plan," 269.
46. Hindmarsh, "Harvard Educational Plan," 174; "Oxford and the Harvard House Plan," *American Oxonian*, January 1931, 64–65.
47. "Oxford and the Harvard House Plan," 64–65.
48. Angell, "College Plan," 262.
49. Pierson, *Yale: The University College*, 411–12; Bergin, *Yale's Residential Colleges*, 35.
50. Perkins, "Impersonal Oxford," 245–47; Lloyd, "Ideas of a University," 85.
51. Hale, "Madness at New Haven," 9–11; White, *A Yale Man*, 66.
52. Lowell, "Self-Education in Harvard College," 70; R. Smith, *Harvard Century*, 228.
53. Pierson, *Yale: The University College*, 420–21.
54. Fraser, *Colleges of the Future*, 393; "Education Bricks and Mortar"; MacLeish, *The Next Harvard*, 46–48.
55. R. Smith, *Harvard Century*, 95; Synnott, *Half-Opened Door*, 111–12.
56. Pierson, *Yale: The University College*, 134–35, 312.
57. Kelley, *Yale*, 448.
58. Synnott, *Half-Opened Door*, 113, 122–23.
59. Kelley, *Yale*, 448; Bergin, *Yale's Residential Colleges*, 120.
60. Jencks and Riesman, "Patterns of Residential Education," 761.
61. Student Council Report of 1931, quoted in Harvard University Committee, "General Education in Harvard College," 235; "General Education in Harvard College," 234; Riesman, "Educational Reform at Harvard College," 768.
62. Riesman, "Education at Harvard," 297–98; Jencks and Riesman, "Pat-

terns of Residential Education," 762; Riesman, "Educational Reform at Harvard College," 347.

63. Riesman, "Education at Harvard," 33–36.
64. Bergin, *Yale's Residential Colleges*, 60–64.
65. Bergin, *Yale's Residential Colleges*, 120.
66. President's Report-Report of the President of Harvard College and Reports of Departments, 9.
67. Bergin, *Yale's Residential Colleges*, 120; Jencks and Riesman, "Patterns of Residential Education," 753.

5
Claremont: The "Oxford Plan of the Pacific"

1. B. Clark, *Higher Education System*, 82; Astin, "Students," 397.
2. Santayana, "Persons and Places," 85.
3. Lyon, *History of Pomona College*, xv; Thelin, "California and the Colleges: Part II," 235–40. The University of California's Southern Branch, which later became the University of California, Los Angeles, was not established until 1923.
4. Lyon, *History of Pomona College*, 17–19.
5. Lyon, *History of Pomona College*, 128, 85, 166.
6. Clary, *Claremont Colleges*, 1, 2; Lyon, *History of Pomona College*, 232, 192.
7. Blaisdell, "Modern College—a Forecast," in Pomona College Papers, 10; James A. Blaisdell to Dr. George S. Sumner, December 1941, quoted in Clary, *Claremont Colleges*, 71.
8. Clary, *Claremont Colleges*, 2; Lyon, *History of Pomona College*, 232.
9. Lyon, *History of Pomona College*, 263–64.
10. Lyon, *History of Pomona College*, 114–16.
11. Blaisdell, "Modern College—a Forecast," 8; Lyon, *History of Pomona College*, 114–15.
12. Lyon, *History of Pomona College*, 233. See Wells, *Oxford and Oxford Life*.
13. Blaisdell, President's Report—Claremont Colleges, 2 January 1936, quoted in Bernard, *Unfinished Dream*, 9.
14. Eaton, *Historical Sketches of Beloit College*, 149.
15. Bernard, *Unfinished Dream*, 5.
16. McNab, *Development of Higher Education in Ontario*, 255–57.
17. McNab, *Development of Higher Education in Ontario*, 259; Ross, "Establishment of the Ph.D. at Toronto," 368–73; Malcolm Wallace to James A. Blaisdell, 8 June 1930, Blaisdell Papers.

18. *University of Toronto*, 17, 31.

19. Blaisdell, President's Report—Claremont Colleges, January 2, 1936, 8.

20. Clary, *Claremont Colleges*, 1; Lyon, *History of Pomona College*, 244–45, 232; Blaisdell, "The Modern College—a Forecast," 6.

21. James A. Blaisdell, "Preliminary Statement, 15 March 1925," in Bernard, *Unfinished Dream*, 8–9.

22. Blaisdell, "Preliminary Statement," 8–9.

23. Blaisdell, "The Modern College—a Forecast," 6; Blaisdell, President's Report—Claremont Colleges, 2 January 1936," in Bernard, *Unfinished Dream*, 9, 8.

24. Blaisdell, President's Report, 8.

25. Blaisdell, "Preliminary Statement," 10; Lyon, *History of Pomona College*, 155–59.

26. Thelin, "California and the Colleges," 154; E. H. Kennard, "Which Way Pomona?" *Pomona Quarterly Magazine*, March 1925, as quoted in Lyon, *History of Pomona College*, 234–35; Savage, "Claremont Colleges Plan," 44; George Marston, "Dedication of Harper Hall," 19 February 1931, Blaisdell Papers, Claremont, Calif.; Stephenson, "Claremont Colleges," 118.

27. Lyon, *History of Pomona College*, 233.

28. Larson and Palmer, *Architectural Planning of the American College*, 70–71; Lyon, *History of Pomona College*, 249.

29. Clary, *Claremont Colleges*, 18; Lyon, *History of Pomona College*, 243–44.

30. Clary, *Claremont Colleges*, 19, 9.

31. Bernard, *Unfinished Dream*, 34.

32. Thelin, *Higher Education and Its Useful Past*, 64.

33. Clary, *Claremont Colleges*, 15, 22–23.

34. Malcolm Wallace to James A. Blaisdell, 8 June 1930, Blaisdell Papers.

35. Lyon, *History of Pomona College*, 382–83; James Blaisdell to George S. Sumner, December 1941, as quoted in Clary, *Claremont Colleges*, 69–71; Lyon, "English Precedents in the Associated Colleges at Claremont," 76.

36. Clary, *Claremont Colleges*, 27, viii.

37. James Blaisdell to J. C. Harper, 26 February 1931, quoted in Clary, *Claremont Colleges*, 29.

38. Clary, *Claremont Colleges*, 58–76, 102.

39. Clary, *Claremont Colleges*, 108.

40. Lyon, *History of Pomona College*, 525; Clary, *Claremont Colleges*, viii.

41. Louis T. Benezet, quoted in McHenry, "Academic Organizational Matrix at Santa Cruz," 95.

6
The University of California, Santa Cruz: "The City on a Hill"

1. Long Range Development Plan University of California, Santa Cruz (September 1963), 12; McHenry, "Academic Organizational Matrix at Santa Cruz," 86. In 1966, Oxford and Cambridge each enrolled about 9,800 students (Mountford, *British Universities*, 167).
2. Ravitch, *Troubled Crusade*, 13-14.
3. Ravitch, *Troubled Crusade*, 14-15; Best, "Revolution of Markets and Management," 187.
4. Leslie F. Robbins, Division of Higher Education, U.S. Department of Health, Education and Welfare, Washington, D.C., letter, May 27, 1964, as quoted in Mayhew, "New Colleges," 1-2.
5. Ravitch, *Troubled Crusade*, 14-15; Kerr, *Uses of the University*, 6.
6. Kerr, *Uses of the University*, 1-45.
7. In *Emergence of the American University*, Veysey argued that the creation of a standard bureaucratic structure between 1870 and 1910 enabled universities to maintain disparate priorities without disintegrating. Kerr, *Uses of the University*, 18.
8. Austen, "Of Size and Quality," 398.
9. Gaff, "Cluster College Concept," 16-17. Gaff noted forty-four cluster colleges at twenty-four institutions. In 1974, Miami University of Ohio established its School of Interdisciplinary Studies, a cluster college of 350 students.
10. See Meiklejohn, *Experimental College;* Brennan, "The Making of a Liberal College," 569-98; Dzuback, *Robert Maynard Hutchins;* Hutchins, *Higher Learning in America.*
11. Veysey, "Stability and Experiment in the American Undergraduate Curriculum," 106.
12. Dzuback, *Robert Maynard Hutchins*, 100-103.
13. Hutchins, *Higher Learning in America*, 59-83.
14. Dzuback, *Robert Maynard Hutchins*, 124-34.
15. Handlin and Handlin, *American College and American Culture*, 79.
16. Grant and Riesman, *Perpetual Dream*, 40-76.
17. Kerr, *Uses of the University*, 18; McHenry, "Idea of the University," 96.
18. Martin, "Stalkers of Meaning," 367-68.
19. McHenry, "Academic Organizational Matrix at Santa Cruz," 91-92, 94. "Just as the cluster of colleges at Claremont, California, forty years ago looked to Oxford for a pattern on which to cut its future, many colleges and universities in the United States have in recent years turned

to the Claremont Colleges for the guidance they seek in trying to bring together the advantages of bigness and smallness" (Herbert R. Kells and Clifford D. Stewart, "The Conference on Cluster College Concept: Introduction," in Kells and Stewart, *Journal of Higher Education* 38 [October 1967]: 357).

20. Hannah, "University as a Matrix," 386.
21. Kells and Stewart, "Conference on Cluster College Concept," 362.
22. Newcomb, "Student Peer-Group Influence," 486.
23. Gaff, "Cluster College Concept," 16–17.
24. Astin, "Students," 397.
25. Ring, "Evaluation for Santa Cruz," 186.
26. Stadtman, *University of California*, 382.
27. Von der Muhll, "University of California at Santa Cruz," 54; McHenry, "Academic Organizational Matrix at Santa Cruz," 87.
28. McHenry, "Academic Organizational Matrix at Santa Cruz," 88.
29. McHenry, "Small College Programs," 32, 33.
30. Von der Muhll, "University of California at Santa Cruz," 66–67. The expression "city on a hill" comes from Jesus Christ's admonition that "a city that is set on a hill cannot be hid"—that is, it can serve as an example to the rest of the world.
31. Grant and Riesman, *Perpetual Dream*, 263; Von der Muhll, "University of California at Santa Cruz," 64–65; Long Range Development Plan University of California, Santa Cruz, 21.
32. Long Range Development Plan University of California, Santa Cruz, 24.
33. *First Twenty Years;* McHenry, "Academic Organizational Matrix at Santa Cruz," 101–2, 178.
34. McHenry, "Academic Organizational Matrix at Santa Cruz," 94–95; Grant and Riesman, *Perpetual Dream*, 256.
35. Academic Quality at Santa Cruz: Report of the Chancellor's Self-Study / Accrediting Committee (Santa Cruz,1976), 30.
36. McHenry, "Academic Organizational Matrix at Santa Cruz," 111–12.
37. Grant and Riesman, *Perpetual Dream*, 76–134.
38. Grant and Riesman, *Perpetual Dream*, 273ff; Riesman, *On Higher Education*, 209–10.
39. Riesman, *On Higher Education*, 209.
40. Von der Muhll, "University of California at Santa Cruz," 69; Kerr, *Uses of the University*, 167.
41. McHenry, "Academic Organizational Matrix at Santa Cruz," 107–8.
42. Academic Quality at Santa Cruz, 30, 37.
43. Riesman, *On Higher Education:* 210; Ring, "Evaluation for Santa Cruz,"

210-12; Gerlertner, *Santa Cruz: The Dream School,* 44; Woodring, *Higher Learning in America,* 209-10.

44. Dressel, "Curriculum and Instruction, 394.

45. Von der Muhll, "University of California at Santa Cruz," 78-79.

46. McHenry, "Academic Organizational Matrix at Santa Cruz," 105.

47. Ring, "Evaluation for Santa Cruz," 209; Report of the Western Association of Schools and Colleges Accrediting Committee, 2; D. Davis, "Cluster College Revisited," 19.

48. Von der Muhll, "University of California at Santa Cruz," 83-85.

49. Fiske, *Guide to Colleges,* 118-19.

50. Report of the Student Union Task Force on the Role of the Colleges, 16; Birnbach, *New and Improved College Book,* 71; Report of the Task Group on Institutional Relationships with Fraternities and Sororities (Santa Cruz, 1986).

Conclusion

1. McHenry, "Academic Organizational Matrix at Santa Cruz," 109.

BIBLIOGRAPHY

Letters and Papers

James A. Blaisdell Papers, Honnold Library, Claremont, California
  James A. Blaisdell Papers (Collected folio, 1926).
  Malcolm Wallace to James A. Blaisdell, 8 June 1930.
  Dedication of Harper Hall, 18 February 1931.
Nathan Pusey Library, Harvard University
  Education Bricks and Mortar. President and Fellows Report of 1949,
    Harvard University, 1949.
  President's Report–Report of the President of Harvard College and
    Reports of Departments, 1954–55.
Special Collections, University of California, Santa Cruz
  Academic Quality at Santa Cruz: Report of the Chancellor's Self-
    Study/Accrediting Committee. Santa Cruz, 1976.
  The First Twenty Years: Two Decades of Building at UCSC. Santa Cruz,
    1986.
  Long Range Development Plan University of California, Santa Cruz.
    Santa Cruz, September 1963.
  McHenry, Dean E., "The Idea of the University." Address given to the
    Carolyn Benton Cockefair Chair in Continuing Education, Univer-
    sity of Missouri, Kansas City, 13 December 1967.
  Report of the Student Union Task Force on the Role of the Colleges.
    Santa Cruz, 1986.
  Report of the Task Group on Institutional Relationships with Fra-
    ternities and Sororities. Santa Cruz, 1986.
  Report of the Western Association of Schools and Colleges Accredit-
    ing Committee. Santa Cruz, 1981.

Books and Periodicals

Adams, Charles Francis. "The Ideal College Organization." *Harvard
  Graduate's Magazine,* September 1907, 202–3.

Alexander, Michael Van Cleave. *The Growth of English Education, 1348–1648: A Social and Cultural History*. University Park: Pennsylvania State University Press, 1990.

"An American at Oxford." *Harvard Graduate's Magazine*, December 1902, 320–21.

Angell, James Rowland. *American Education: Addresses and Articles*. New York: Books for Universities Press, 1970.

Arnold, Matthew. *Culture and Anarchy: An Essay in Political and Social Criticism*. Vol. 7 of *Complete Prose Works of Matthew Arnold*. London: Macmillan, 1903.

———. *Essays in Criticism, First Series*. Vol. 3 of *Complete Prose Works of Matthew Arnold*. London: Macmillan, 1903.

Astin, Alexander. "Students" in "Curriculum and Instruction." In "The Conference on Cluster College Concept," ed. Herbert R. Kells and Clifford T. Stewart, *Journal of Higher Education* 38 (October 1967): 396–97.

Attwater, Aubrey. *Pembroke College, Cambridge: A Short History*. Cambridge: The University Press, 1893.

Austen, C. Grey. "Of Size and Quality." In "The Conference on Cluster College Concept," ed. Herbert R. Kells and Clifford T. Stewart, *Journal of Higher Education* 38 (October 1967): 398–400.

Aydelotte, Frank. *The American Rhodes Scholars: A Review of the First Forty Years*. Princeton: Princeton University Press, 1946.

———. *The Oxford Stamp and Other Essays: Articles from the Educational Creed of an American Oxonian*. New York: Oxford University Press, 1917.

Baker, Ray Stannard. *Woodrow Wilson: Life and Letters*. Garden City, N.Y.: Doubleday, Page, 1939.

Beale, Joseph H. "Reorganization of the University." *Harvard Graduate's Magazine*, September 1907, 31–37.

Beerbohm, Max. *Zuleika Dobson: or An Oxford Love Story*. London: William Heinemann, 1911.

Bergin, Thomas G. *Yale's Residential Colleges: The First Fifty Years*. New Haven: Yale University Press, 1983.

Bernard, Robert J. *An Unfinished Dream: A Chronicle of the Group Plan of the Claremont Colleges*. Claremont, Calif.: Claremont Colleges, 1982.

Best, John Hardin. "The Revolution of Markets and Management." *History of Education Quarterly* 28 (Summer 1988): 177–90.

Bill, E. G. W., and Mason, J. F. A. *Christ Church and Reform: 1850–1867*. Oxford: Clarendon, 1970.

Birnbach, Lisa. *Lisa Birnbach's New and Improved College Book*. Englewood Cliffs, N.J.: Prentice-Hall, 1990.

Block, Jean. *The Uses of Gothic: Planning and Building the Campus of the University of Chicago*. Chicago: University of Chicago Library, 1983.

Bolles, Frank. "An Administrative Problem." *Harvard Graduate's Magazine*, September 1894, 1–8.

Bragdon, Henry Wilkinson. *Woodrow Wilson: The Academic Years*. Cambridge: Belknap Press of Harvard University Press, 1967.

Brennan, Robert Thomas. "The Making of the Liberal College: Alexander Meiklejohn at Amherst." *History of Education Quarterly* 28 (Winter 1988): 569–98.

Bristed, Charles Astor. *Five Years in an English University*. New York: G. P. Putnam, 1952.

Brooke, Christopher, and Highfield, Roger. *Oxford and Cambridge*. Cambridge: Cambridge University Press, 1987.

Brown, Rollo Walter. *Dean Briggs*. New York: Harper and Brothers, 1926.

Brubacher, John S., and Rudy, Willis. *Higher Education in Transition: A History of American Colleges and Universities, 1636–1976*. New York: Harper and Row, 1976.

Buchloh, Paul G., and Rix, Walter, eds. *American Colony of Göttingen: Historical and Other Data Collected Between the Years 1855 and 1888*. Göttingen, Germany: Göttingen University, 1976.

Burton, D. H. "Theodore Roosevelt and the 'Special Relationship' with Britain." *History Today* 23 (August 1973): 528–35.

Canby, Henry Seidel. *Alma Mater: The Gothic Age of the American College*. New York: Farrar and Rinehart, 1936.

Clark, Burton R. *The Higher Education System: Academic Organization in Cross-National Perspective*. Berkeley: University of California Press, 1983.

———. "The Organizational Saga in Higher Education." *Administrative Science Quarterly* 17 (June 1972): 178–184.

Clark, Kenneth. *The Gothic Revival: An Essay on the History of Taste*. New York: Scribners, 1950.

Clary, William W. *The Claremont Colleges: A History of the Development of the Claremont Group Plan*. Claremont, Calif.: Claremont University Center, 1970.

Cobban, Alan B. *The Medieval English Universities*. Berkeley: University of California Press, 1988.

Coffin, Robert P. Tristam. "The Paradox of Oxford." In *College Years:*

Essays of College Life, ed. Joseph Bunn Heidler. New York: R. Long and R. R. Smith, 1933.

Coleman, Peter J. *Progressivism and the World of Social Reform: New Zealand and the Origins of the American Welfare State*. Lawrence: University Press of Kansas, 1987.

Commager, Henry Steele. *Britain Through American Eyes*. New York: McGraw-Hill, 1974.

Copleston, Edward. *A Reply to the Calumnies Against Oxford by the Edinburgh Review*. Oxford, 1810.

Corbin, John A. *Which College for the Boy? Leading Types in American Education*. Boston: Houghton-Mifflin, 1908.

———. *An American at Oxford*. Boston: Houghton-Mifflin, 1902.

Cowley, W. H. "European Influences upon American Higher Education." *Educational Record* 20 (April 1939): 165-90.

———. "The History of College Residential Housing I." *School and Society* 40 (December 1, 1934) 705-12.

———. "The History of College Residential Housing II." *School and Society* 40 (December 8, 1934): 758-64.

Craig, Hardin. *Woodrow Wilson at Princeton*. Norman: University of Oklahoma Press, 1960).

Cram, Ralph Adams. *The Significance of Gothic Art*. Boston: Marshall Jones, 1918.

———. *The Ministry of Art*. Boston: Houghton-Mifflin, 1910.

Curtis, Mark H. *Oxford and Cambridge in Transition: An Essay on the Changing Relations Between the English Universities and English Society*. Oxford: Clarendon, 1959.

Davis, David J. "The Cluster College Revisited: A Dream Falls on Hard Times." *College Teaching* 33, no.1 (1985): 15-20.

Davis, H. W. Carless. *A History of Balliol College*. Oxford: F. E. Robinson and Co., 1963.

Dressel, Paul L. "Curriculum and Instruction." In "The Conference on the Cluster College Concept," ed. Herbert R. Kells and Clifford T. Stewart, *Journal of Higher Education* 38 (October 1967): 393-96.

Dzuback, Mary Ann. *Robert Maynard Hutchins: Portrait of an Educator*. Chicago: University of Chicago Press, 1991.

Eaton, Edward Dwight. *Historical Sketches of Beloit College*. New York: A. S. Barnes and Co., 1935.

Emden, A. B. *An Oxford Hall in Medieval Times*. Oxford: Clarendon, 1924.

Engel, A. J. *From Clergyman to Don: The Rise of the Academic Profession in Nineteenth-Century Oxford.* Oxford: Clarendon, 1983.

"Essays on a Professional Education by R. L. Edgeworth." *Edinburgh Review* 15 (October 1809): 40-42.

Feldman, Penny Hollander. *Recruiting an Elite: Admission to Harvard College.* New York: Garland, 1988.

Fiske, Edward B. *The Fiske Guide to Colleges.* New York: Times Books, 1989.

Flexner, Abraham. *The American College: A Criticism.* New York: Century, 1908.

Fowler, Thomas. *The History of Corpus Christi College with a List of its Members.* Oxford: Oxford Historical Society, 1893.

Fraser, Mowat G. *The Colleges of the Future: An Appraisal of Fundamental Plans and Trends in Higher Education.* New York: Columbia University Press, 1937.

Gaff, Jerry R. "The Cluster College Concept." In *The Cluster College,* ed. Jerry R. Gaff and associates. San Francisco: Jossey-Bass, 1970.

Garland, Martha McMakin. *Cambridge Before Darwin: The Idea of a Liberal Education, 1800-1860.* Cambridge: Cambridge University Press, 1980.

Geiger, Roger. *To Advance Knowledge: The Growth of American Research Universities, 1900-1940.* New York: Oxford University Press, 1986.

Gerlertner, Carey Q. *Santa Cruz: The Dream School of the Sixties—Twelve Years Later.* (Thesis, University of California, Berkeley,1977).

Gilman, Daniel Coit. *University Problems in the United States.* New York: The Century Co., 1898.

Grant, Gerald, and Riesman, David. *The Perpetual Dream: Reform and Experiment in the American College.* Chicago: University of Chicago Press, 1978.

Haines, IV, George. "Second Reform of Cambridge and Oxford." In *Essays on German Influence upon English Education and Science, 1850-1919,* ed.George Haines IV. Hamden, Conn.: Connecticut College, 1969.

Hale, William Harlan. "The Madness at New Haven." *The Harkness Hoot: A Yale Undergraduate Review,* April-May 1931, 9-11.

Hamilton, Sir William. "Universities of England—Oxford." *Edinburgh Review* 53 (June 1831): 384-427.

Hamlin, A. D. F. "Educational Influence of Collegiate Architecture." *Architectural Forum* 43 (December 1925): 321-26.

Handlin, Oscar, and Handlin, Mary F. *The American College and American Culture: Socialization as a Function of Higher Education.* New York: McGraw-Hill, 1970.

Hannah, John A. "The University as a Matrix." In "The Conference on the Cluster College Concept," ed. Herbert R. Kells and Clifford T. Stewart, *Journal of Higher Education* 38 (October 1967): 378–89.

Harris, W. T. "Oxford University and the Rhodes Scholarships." Proceedings and Addresses of the National Educational Association, 1903, 263–78.

Hart, Albert Bushnell. "The Critic's, and the Real Harvard." *Boston Evening Transcript*, September 28, 1907, sec. 3, 1.

Harvard University Committee on the Objectives of a General Education in a Free Society. *General Education in a Free Society: Report of the Harvard Committee.* Cambridge, Mass., 1945.

Hawes, James Anderson. *Twenty Years Among the Twenty Year Olds: A Story of Our Colleges of Today.* New York: E. P. Dutton, 1929.

Hill, George Birkbeck. *Harvard College by an Oxonian.* New York: Macmillan, 1894.

Hindmarsh, Albert E. "A Harvard Educational Plan." *Journal of Higher Education* 3 (April 1932): 171–78.

Hodgskin, Thomas. *Travels in the North of Germany, Describing the Present State of the Social and Political Institutions.* Edinburgh, 1820.

Honey, John R. de S. *Tom Brown's Universe: The Development of Victorian Public Schools.* London: Willington, 1977.

Horn, Francis, et al. "Facilities and Learning: An Overview of Development." In *Higher Education: Some Newer Developments,* ed. Samuel Baskin. New York: McGraw-Hill, 1965.

Hutchins, Robert Maynard. *The Higher Learning in America.* New Haven: Yale University Press, 1936.

"Irish and English Universities." *Dublin Review* 1 (May 1836): 47–67.

Jencks, Christopher, and Riesman, David. "Patterns of Residential Education: A Case Study of Harvard." In *The American College: A Psychological and Social Interpretation of the Higher Learning,* ed. Nevitt Sanford. New York: John Wiley, 1962.

Jones, Edward Safford. *Comprehensive Examinations in American Colleges.* New York: Macmillan, 1933.

Kaestle, Carl. *Pillars of the Republic: Common Schools and American Society, 1780–1860.* New York: Hill and Wang, 1983.

Kearney, Hugh. *Scholars and Gentlemen: Universities and Society in Pre-*

Industrial Britain, 1500–1700. Ithaca, N.Y.: Cornell University Press, 1970.

Kelley, Brooks Mather. *Yale, A History.* New Haven: Yale University Press, 1974.

Kerr, Clark. *The Uses of the University,* 3rd edition. Cambridge: Harvard University Press, 1982.

Larson, Jens F., and Palmer, Archie M. *Architectural Planning of the American College.* New York: McGraw-Hill, 1933.

Lawson, John, and Silver, Harold. *A Social History of Education in England.* London: Methuen and Co., 1973.

Leacock, Stephen. *My Discovery of England.* London: Dodd, Mead, 1922.

Leitch, Alexander. *A Princeton Companion.* Princeton: Princeton University Press, 1978.

Leslie, W. Bruce. *Gentlemen and Scholars: College and Community in the "Age of the University", 1865–1917.* University Park: Pennsylvania State University Press, 1992.

Link, Arthur S. *Wilson: The Road to the White House.* Princeton: Princeton University Press, 1947.

Lipset, Seymour Martin. "Political Controversies at Harvard, 1636–1974." In *Education and Politics at Harvard: Two Essays Prepared for the Carnegie Commission on Higher Education,* ed. Seymour Martin Lipset and David Riesman. New York: McGraw-Hill, 1975.

Lloyd, David Demarest. "The Ideas of a University: Cambridge Values and Harvard System." *Harvard Graduate's Magazine,* 41, n. 97 (1932–33): 85–98.

Lowe, Roy. "Anglo-Americanism in the Planning of Universities in the United States." *History of Education* 15 (1986): 247–59.

Lowell, Abbot Lawrence. "English Precedents in the Associated Colleges at Claremont." *American Oxonian,* April 1948, 76–80.

———. *At War with Academic Tradition.* Cambridge: Harvard University Press, 1934.

———. "Self-Education in Harvard College" *Journal of Higher Education* 2 (February 1930): 65–72.

———. "General Examinations and Tutors in Harvard College." *Educational Record* 8, n. 2 (1927): 61–84.

———. "The Higher Education and Its Present Task: Formalism in Education in the State University and the New South." In *Inauguration of Harry Woodburn Chase as President of the University of North Carolina.* Chapel Hill, N.C., 1920.

————. "Inaugural Address." *Harvard Graduate's Magazine,* December 1909, 211–23.

————. "Dormitories and College Life." *Harvard Graduate's Magazine,* June 1904, 523–28.

Lyon, E. Wilson. *History of Pomona College, 1887–1969.* Claremont, Calif.: The College, 1977.

————. "Claremont Goes to Oxford." *American Oxonian,* October 1967, 263–68.

Mackail, J. W. *James Leigh Strachan-Davidson.* Oxford: Clarendon, 1925.

Mackenzie, Compton. *Sinister Street.* London: McDonald, 1913.

MacLeish, Archibald. *The Next Harvard, as Seen by Archibald MacLeish.* Cambridge: Harvard University Press, 1941.

Macmillan, Kerr D. "Ideals for an Effective College." *Association of American Colleges Bulletin* 13 (May 1927): 210–26.

Mallet, Charles Edward. *A History of the University of Oxford.* London: Methuen, 1926.

Mangan, J. A. *Athleticism in the Victorian and Edwardian Public School: The Emergence of an Educational Ideology.* London: Cambridge University Press, 1981.

Marrou, Henri-Irénée. *The Meaning of History.* Baltimore: Helicon,1966.

Martin, Warren Bryan. "Stalkers of Meaning." In "The Conference on the Cluster College Concept," ed. Herbert R. Kells and Clifford T. Stewart, *Journal of Higher Education* 38 (October 1967): 363–73.

Mayhew, Lewis B. "The New Colleges." In *Higher Education: Some Newer Developments,* ed. Samuel Baskin. New York: McGraw-Hill, 1965.

McHenry, Dean E. "Academic Organizational Matrix at Santa Cruz." In *Academic Departments: Problems, Variations and Alternatives,* ed. Dean E. McHenry. San Francisco: Jossey-Bass, 1977.

————. "University of California, Santa Cruz." *Architectural Record* 136 (November 1964): 176–85.

————. "Small College Programs for a Large University." *College and University Business,* July 1964, 31–3.

McNab, G. G. *The Development of Higher Education in Ontario.* Toronto: Ryerson, 1925.

Meiklejohn, Alexander. *The Liberal College.* New York: Arno Press, 1969.

————. *The Experimental College.* New York: Harper, 1932.

Morison, Samuel Eliot. *Three Centuries of Harvard: 1636–1936.* Cambridge: Harvard University Press, 1936.

Mountford, Sir James. *British Universities*. Oxford: Oxford University Press, 1966.

Myers, William Starr, ed. *Woodrow Wilson: Some Princeton Memories*. Princeton: Princeton University Press, 1946.

Newcomb, Theodore M. "Student Peer-Group Influence." In *The American College: A Psychological and Social Interpretation of the Higher Learning*, ed. Nevitt Sanford. New York: John Wiley, 1962.

Newman, John Henry. *The Idea of a University*. Oxford, 1976.

Norwich, John J., ed. *Great Architecture of the World*. London: Bonanza, 1975.

Noverr, Douglas A., and Ziewacz, Lawrence E. *The Games They Played: Sports in American History, 1865–1980*. Chicago: McGraw-Hill, 1983.

"Oxford and the Harvard House Plan." *American Oxonian*, January 1931, 64–65.

Parkin, George R. *The Rhodes Scholarships*. Boston: Houghton-Mifflin, 1912.

Peile, John. *Christ's College*. London: J. Clay, 1900.

Perkins, H. P. "The Impersonal Oxford." *Association of American Colleges Bulletin* 16 (May 1930): 245–60

Pierson, George Wilson. *Yale: The University College, 1921–37* New Haven: Yale University Press, 1955.

Polkinghorne, Donald. *Methodology for the Human Sciences: Systems of Inquiry*. Albany: State University of New York Press, 1983.

Pratt, Henry Putnam. "An Undergraduate Plan." *Harvard Graduate's Magazine*, June 1905, 588–92.

Proctor, Mortimer R. *The English University Novel*. Berkeley: University of California Press, 1957.

Ravitch, Diane. *The Troubled Crusade: American Education, 1945–80*. New York: Basic Books, 1983.

Richardson, Leon B. *A Study of the Liberal College*. Hanover, N.H.: Dartmouth College, 1924.

Riesman, David. *On Higher Education: The Academic Enterprise in an Era of Increasing Student Consumerism*. San Francisco: Jossey-Bass, 1980.

———. "Education at Harvard." *Change*, September 1975, 24–48.

———. "Educational Reform at Harvard College: Meritocracy and its Adversaries." In *Education and Politics at Harvard: Two Essays Prepared for the Carnegie Commission on Higher Education*, ed. Seymour Martin Lipset and David Riesman. New York: McGraw-Hill, 1975.

Ring, Lloyd J. "Evaluation for Santa Cruz." In *The New Colleges: Toward an Appraisal,* ed. Paul L. Dressel. Iowa City: American College Testing Program, 1971.

Robertson, C. Grant. *All Souls College.* London: F. E. Robertson, 1899.

Ross, Peter N. "The Establishment of the Ph.D. at Toronto: A Case of American Influence." *History of Education Quarterly* 12 (Fall 1972): 358–80.

Rothblatt, Sheldon. " 'Standing Antagonisms': The Relationship of Undergraduate to Graduate Education." In *The Future of State Universities: Issues in Teaching, Service, and Public Service,* ed. Leslie Koepplin and David Wilson. Elizabeth, N.J.: Rutgers University Press, 1986.

———. *The Revolution of the Dons: Cambridge and Society in Victorian England.* New York: Basic Books, 1968.

Rudolph, Frederick. *Curriculum: A History of the American Undergraduate Course of Study Since 1636.* San Francisco: Jossey-Bass, 1978.

Sanderson, Michael, ed. *The Universities in the Nineteenth Century.* London, 1975.

Santayana, George. "Persons and Places: First Friends at Harvard College." *Atlantic Monthly,* May 1943, 80–86.

Savage, George W. "The Claremont Colleges Plan." *Educational Record* 8 (January 1927): 40–44.

Savath, Edward. "The Education of an Elite." *History of Education Quarterly* 28 (Fall 1988): 367–86.

Scott, Drusilla. *A. D. Lindsay: A Biography.* Oxford: Basil Blackwell, 1971.

Shils, Edward. *Tradition.* Chicago: University of Chicago Press, 1981.

Slosson, Edwin. *Great American Universities.* New York: Macmillan, 1912.

Smith, Adam. *An Inquiry into the Nature and Causes of the Wealth of Nations.* New York: Modern Library, 1937.

Smith, Richard Norton. *The Harvard Century: The Making of a University to a Nation.* New York: Simon and Schuster, 1986.

Stadtman, Verne A. *The University of California, 1868–1968.* Berkeley: University of California Press, 1970.

Stephenson, N. W. "Claremont Colleges." *Journal of Higher Education* 2 (March 1932): 115–20.

Storr, Richard J. *Harper's University: The Beginnings: A History of the University of Chicago.* Chicago: University of Chicago Press, 1966.

Symmonds, Richard. *Oxford and Empire.* New York, 1986.

Synnott, Marcia Graham. *The Half-Opened Door: Discrimination and Admission at Harvard, Yale and Princeton 1900–70.* Westport, Conn.: Greenwood Press, 1979.

Thayer, William Roscoe. "Germanization, Oxfordization and Critics." *Harvard Graduate's Magazine,* December 1907, 275–88.

Thelin, John R. "Retrospective: Laurence Veysey's *The Emergence of the American University.*" *History of Education Quarterly* 27 (Winter 1987): 517–24.

———. *Higher Education and Its Useful Past.* Cambridge: Schenkman, 1982.

———. "California and the Colleges: Part II." *California Historical Review* 56 (Fall 1977): 230–49.

———. "California and the Colleges." *California Historical Review* 56 (Summer 1977): 140–63.

Thompson, James. "The House System." In *President's Report, Decennial Publications of the University of Chicago* 1 (1903): 387–95.

Thwing, Charles Franklin. *The American and German University: One Hundred Years of History.* New York: Macmillan, 1928.

———. *Universities of the World.* New York: Macmillan, 1911.

———. *A History of Higher Education in America.* New York: D. Appleton, 1906.

"Traité de Mechanique Céleste par P.S. La Place." *Edinburgh Review* 11 (January 1808): 249–84.

Turner, Paul Venable. *Campus: An American Planning Tradition.* Cambridge: MIT Press, 1984.

Twombley, John Fogg. "The College Hall System." *Harvard Graduate's Magazine,* June 1905, 584–88.

University of Toronto: The Provincial University of Ontario, 1827–1927: The First 100 Years. Toronto, 1927.

Veysey, Laurence R. "Stability and Experiment in the American Undergraduate Curriculum." In *ASHE Reader on Academic Programs in Colleges and Universities,* ed. Clifton Conrad. Lexington, Mass.: Ginn Press, 1985.

———. *The Emergence of the American University.* Chicago: University of Chicago Press, 1965.

———. "The Academic Mind of Woodrow Wilson." *The Mississippi Valley Historical Review* 49 (March 1963): 613–34.

Von der Muhll, George. "The University of California at Santa Cruz: Institutionalizing Eden in a Changing World." In *Against the Current: Reform and Experiment in Higher Education,* ed. Richard M. Jones and Barbara Leigh Smith. Cambridge: Schenkman, 1984

Wechsler, Harold. "An Academic Gresham's Law: Group Repulsion as a Theme in American Higher Education. *Teacher's College Record* 82 (Summer 1981): 567–88.

———. *The Qualified Student.* New York: John Wiley, 1977.

Wells, J. *Oxford and Oxford Life.* London: Methuen, 1892.

Wenley, R. M. "Reckless Tenants: University of Michigan Phi Beta Kappa Address May 1918." *Educational Review* 47 (January 1919): 22–42.

Wertenbaker, Thomas Jefferson. *Princeton 1746–1896.* Princeton: Princeton University Press, 1946.

West, Andrew. *The Graduate College at Princeton, with Some Reflections on the Humanizing of Learning.* Princeton: Princeton University Press, 1913.

White, Milton. *A Yale Man.* Garden City, N.Y.: Doubleday, 1966.

Wilson, H. A. *Magdalen College.* London: F. E. Robinson, 1899.

Wilson, Woodrow. "What Is a College For?" *Scribner's Magazine,* November 1909. Reprinted in *Woodrow Wilson: College and State,* vol 2., ed. Ray Stannard Baker and William E. Dodd. New York: Harper and Brothers, 1925.

———. "The Spirit of Learning." *Harvard Graduate's Magazine,* September 1909, 1–17.

Wood, Norman. *The Reformation and English Education: A Study of the Influence of Religious Uniformity on English Education in the Sixteenth Century.* London, 1931.

Woodring, Paul. *The Higher Learning in America: A Reassessment.* New York: McGraw-Hill, 1968.

Yeomans, Henry Aaron. *Abbott Lawrence Lowell, 1856–1943.* Cambridge: Harvard University Press, 1948.

Index

culture, 113–18 passim; houses' impact on academic life, 118–20; success of the house system, 121–24

Harvard University houses: Adams House, 107; Kirkland House, 107; Leverett House, 107; Winthrop House, 107; Dunster House, 107, 115; Lowell House, 107, 115; Eliot House, 107, 115, 116

Harvey Mudd College, 140–43. *See also* Claremont Colleges

Hawes, James Anderson, 46, 86–87

Higher Learning in America, 150

Hill, George B. N., 54, 57, 70, 95

Hodgskin, Thomas, 18–19

Hutchins, Robert Maynard, 149–51

Jencks, Christopher, 118, 119–20

Jenkyns, Richard, 35

Jones, Frederick S., 93

Jowett, Benjamin, 35–36, 81

Judson, Harry Pratt, 78

Kaufman, Gordon, 136

Kennard, E. H., 134

Kerr, Clark, 3, 146–47, 157

Leacock, Stephen, 93, 98

Lindsey, A. D., 36, 63, 151

Lloyd, David Demarest, 112

Lowell, Abbott Lawrence: educational concerns, 4, 39–44; champions Oxbridge-influenced reform, 9, 71–72, 90, 94–95; praises English students, 46; ideas shared by others, 54–55; supports mandatory student residence, 68; supports racially restrictive admissions policies, 92–93, 117; assumes Harvard presidency, 95; implements academic reform, 95–97; works to restore residential atmosphere at Harvard, 98–99; accepts Harkness's offer to build house system, 105–6; confidence in house system, 109, 122, 123; concern over house selection methods, 113–14, 121; ideas influential at Claremont, 126, 129, 137; ideas not influential in 1960s, 153, 154

Lyon, E. Wilson, 60, 140

McCosh, James, 79, 82

McHenry, Dean, 144, 152–53, 157–59, 161

MacLeish, Archibald, 115

McMillan, Kerr D., 101, 155

Magdalen College (Oxford), 17

Marston, George, 129, 132, 135

Martin, Warren Bryan, 152–53

May, Ernest, 120

Meiklejohn, Alexander, 148–49

Mendell, Clarence, 105

Merton College (Oxford), 14–15, 115

Morison, Samuel Eliot, 11, 105, 111

Newcomb, Theodore, 155

Newman, John Henry, 6–7, 29–30, 61, 81, 113, 147

Oriel College (Oxford), 19, 22

Oxbridge: impact on American visitors, 5–6; perceived past defined, 11–16; residential college origins, 13–14; residential pattern in middle ages, 13–15; development of collegial governance structure, 16–17; criticized by alumni, 17–18; curricula, 18–20; examination and degree